HIS
HEALING HANDS

HIS
HEALING HANDS

Neil Cosslett

HODDER AND STOUGHTON
LONDON SYDNEY AUCKLAND TORONTO

British Library Cataloguing in Publication Data

Cosslett, Neil
   His healing hands. – (Hodder Christian
   paperback)
   1. Spiritual healing
   I. Title
   615.8'52   RZ400

   ISBN 0 340 36865 9

CONTENTS

PREFACE AND ACKNOWLEDGEMENTS

At a time when it is marvellous that there are now so many books available about exciting developments in Christian healing ministry, you might well wonder why there should be another. What I have been keen to produce is something a little different. My simple aim is to encourage ordinary Christians and churches everywhere to accept this ministry and to use it as a vital part of Christian life today.

I am therefore writing for ordinary Christian people – members, leaders or ministers – who belong to ordinary Christian churches, to offer just a glimpse of how the ministry of Christian healing can quickly develop and then transform the life and ministry of a church, bringing a new appreciation of God's great love and care for his people and a deeper understanding of the power of real prayer together.

Whilst you will not find pages full of incredible miracles or the story of a successful church, what you will find is straightforward guidance for newcomers to the healing part of our Christian ministry, illustrated by many small but wonderful acts of healing by a loving Father, and also other moments of heartache and seeming failure. This book has been written in order to offer real help and encouragement to all who want to know more about what is involved in stepping into Christian healing ministry.

With this broad aim in view, I offer a basic introduction to many aspects of Christian healing ministry today. I have taken a brief look at the nature of God's love and his longing for healing for his children, the calling of his Church to continue Christ's ministry of healing and then the various ways in which we can respond to that calling in our ordinary daily ministry.

All of this is set in the context of the life and ministry of a small church in a big city where, as a cautious vicar, I have had to learn to grow in faith and understanding one step at a time. Whilst all of my current illustrations stem from experiences we have shared at St Mark's, I have benefited greatly from the writings and guidance of many others and this is bound to be reflected throughout these chapters. I have listed in appendix 2 books and pamphlets I would recommend for those who wish to pursue these areas more deeply than the scope and size of this book permits. For those who would like to use the book as a basis for group study, in appendix 1 I have suggested some questions for discussion.

It is my dream that one day Christian churches everywhere will see, accept and use the healing power of Christ as a part of their everyday ministry and thus grow in faith, expectancy and love. This book is written as a contribution towards the realisation of that dream.

I suppose I am a rather reluctant writer. I had never imagined that I should be called upon to write a book, nor that I should have the privilege of three months' sabbatical leave in which to produce it. Such a task could not have been completed without a great deal of help and encouragement from many other people to whom I owe much gratitude.

So many of our friends in our church family at St Mark's have been of tremendous support, not only with much practical help and encouragement but also with their faithful prayers throughout the preparation of this book. Many have allowed me to share parts of their personal lives with you – not always an easy thing to do – though all names have been changed to protect each one's privacy.

Bishop David Sheppard encouraged and enabled me to take this sabbatical leave and, together with Bishop Bill Flagg, gave the early advice and direction that I needed. Revd John Richards, an Anglican representative on the Church's Council of Health and Healing, has been of continuous support throughout the preparation and writing with much clear guidance, constructive criticism and helpful suggestion.

Barbara and Jim Canning have been immensely kind in offering us a peaceful place of retreat, which my family and I have grown to love during our time here, an experience we shall never forget. And finally I mention my wife Jenny, for all her patience and encouragement as she has read through and corrected the drafts of these chapters, and my children, Kerry, David and Wendy, for being so understanding whilst Dad has had to do his writing!

To all I have mentioned, and to others who have helped in the production of this book, I offer deep and sincere thanks. I pray that many will be guided, encouraged and healed as a result of this combined effort.

Neil Cosslett
July 1983
Frome, Somerset

Chapter 1

'DO NOT BE AFRAID . . .'

A Personal Testimony

New Year's Eve had drawn to its close. We were just two hours into 1982 and I was getting undressed to go to bed, feeling tired but happy at the thought of the new year that lay ahead. Little did I imagine what 1982 had in store for us all.

As I was getting ready for bed I noticed that my right arm seemed a little stiff. I reckoned I must have strained it with all the lifting we had been doing. Then I noticed a large lump under my arm – I hadn't felt that before. Still, it would probably be better in a day or two. I tumbled into bed and was soon fast asleep.

A few days later the swelling was still there and my arm felt worse if anything. I went to see my doctor. He confirmed that it appeared to be a strain and warned me to take it easy with my right arm. The lump under my arm was a swollen gland, probably due to the strain. I took things fairly easily for a couple of weeks, but there was no improvement. One morning, I had to take my son to see the doctor and while there I mentioned my arm again. He took another look and suggested I should see a specialist about it.

The appointment was made and a few weeks later I was being examined at a local clinic. The specialist searched for a cut or scratch on my arm which might have caused the gland to swell. For once there was none. Instead he became interested in a small birthmark on my arm. I was puzzled at the attention he was giving to it. I remembered that the previous summer it had caused me quite a bit of irritation in the sunshine but I had had no trouble since. Could this have caused the gland to swell? After a little thought he suggested that the offending gland ought to be removed and asked whether I would be willing to spend a few days in hospital. I agreed.

The card from the hospital arrived in no time at all. I was to be admitted on the Monday before Ash Wednesday, which I felt was a nuisance because we were having another day of prayer and an evening service of praise and prayer for healing. I phoned the hospital to ask whether I could be out by the Wednesday. They couldn't say, so the Ash Wednesday programme was planned on the assumption that I would not be there.

On the Monday I was admitted to a ward for up to five-day patients only and on the Tuesday the gland was to be removed. I felt rather nervous for although the hospital was familiar ground, I had not been a hospital patient since I was a child. Still, it was to be a relatively small operation and would all be over by the weekend.

When the specialist came around he informed me of a change of plan. He had decided to remove the birthmark on my arm first, to see whether it could be the cause of the swollen gland. Then, if necessary, he would remove the gland later in the week. I was encouraged. Perhaps I would not need to have the gland removed after all. Inwardly I began to realise how frightened I really was about having the operation to remove the gland and I began to pray that God would heal me without surgery being necessary.

The operation to remove the birthmark was only a minor affair. I felt quite calm throughout the operation which was performed with a local anaesthetic, and felt encouraged to be back in the ward again so soon. I then had to wait for the results of tests before any further decision was made.

Ash Wednesday arrived. I wished I was outside and free to be with everyone else at St Mark's. I had my own little day of prayer lying on the hospital bed, but most of my prayers were the constant repetition: 'Please may the gland be healed, Lord, without surgery.' When evening came, after my wife and the other visitors had left to return for the service in church, I lay down on my bed, closed my eyes and tried hard to imagine I was there with them. Eventually I could picture various members of the congregation going forward for prayers for healing with laying on of hands. And then, as I lay there, I experienced something quite incredible. It was the feeling of many hands being laid on *my* head. It was beautiful, so calming, and it began to fill me with a deep sense of peace. I had received the laying on of hands on quite a number of occasions before, but it was never like this. I would probably have been lying there in this rather blissful peacefulness for quite a time, had not chaos broken out on the ward. Two of the nurses' handbags had been stolen through a window, the police had arrived and there was to be little peace on the ward for the rest of the evening.

The next day Ann Barnett, our Deaconess, came to see me to tell me all about the events of Ash Wednesday and I shared with her my own experience at the time of the service. Her response made my eyes water, for apparently member after member of the congregation had come forward to receive laying on of hands for my healing. Even the young choir members had come forward 'for Neil'. I felt very humbled after my self-centred day of prayer. However, I still continued to pray and to believe that further surgery would not now be necessary.

It was late on the Thursday when the ward doctor came with the results of the operation. The small mark on my arm had turned out to be a melanoma, he explained. 'What's that?' I asked. His face fell; that was clearly the question he was hoping that I wouldn't ask. 'It's a type of skin tumour,' was his reply. I could sense by his tone that it was pretty serious but there was no time to ask any more just then. It seemed strange really, for I had in the past met so many people with minor complaints who had mistakenly convinced themselves that they had cancer. Now here I was in hospital, never imagining that my little complaint could have been a tumour. In my life I had grown used to coping with shocks and I reacted with an overpowering feeling of sadness. It felt as if I had begun the last chapter of my life.

Next morning I was cheered a little with the news that I could go home for the weekend. I had to be back in another ward on Monday morning to be ready for the operation to remove the gland on the Tuesday. I was still not sure just how serious my problem was, so I decided to keep the news to myself for the time being. We had a lovely weekend together as a family: a visit to the cinema on the Saturday and then the fellowship and worship of Sunday with an afternoon visit to a local park. My wife noticed the great cloud of sadness that hung over me but thought it was probably due to the prospect of the coming operation. As I watched the children playing happily I was filled with regret for the comparatively small amount of time I spent with them and I wondered whether I would live to see them grow up. Somehow, at the time, I doubted it.

The new ward seemed to have a rather special feel about it. The ward sister was a committed Christian who really had set her mark on the place and I felt encouraged to be in such surroundings. She was also very patient in coping with the steady stream of visitors – parishioners and other friends – who came to see me. Tuesday's operation was to be postponed until Friday when the offending gland would be removed, and possibly other glands as well. Meanwhile, a number of other tests would be necessary to see whether the trouble had spread. All of these tests were to prove negative.

By now, in my self-preoccupied prayer times, I was beginning to ask many questions. I had known that God could heal the gland without surgery and I had believed he would. But he hadn't. I couldn't understand why, for I would certainly have given clear testimony to such a healing and it would have been a great witness to his healing power. What was he playing at? We were supposed to have a healing ministry at St Mark's and here was I – the vicar – in hospital with cancer. This was the beginning of a battle between faith and fear. Fear was bringing all kinds of doubts and worries and a great deal of self-centredness; faith was calling me simply to trust in God. It was to be a fierce battle.

A spell in hospital offers plenty of time for thinking and

praying. I would often lie on my bed and think about what I was missing: my family and home, St Mark's and all our friends there, the freedom of just being able to walk about and see the trees and flowers and grass. I felt rather sorry for myself. Sometimes I would go over to chat with other patients and I always felt better afterwards. I was thinking about this one day when I began to realise that if God had allowed me to be there, then there must be things that he wanted me to do. From then on I spent much more time doing what I could to see other patients on the ward. I had often in the past visited people in hospital, but now it was different. For the first time I could really understand their situation and their feelings, for I shared them. As I became less preoccupied with my own troubles, so my faith began to gain the upper hand over my fears, especially with the encouraging results of all the tests.

In one of my prayer times that week, I imagined I could see Jesus in the distance. He was surrounded by many people in black and I wanted to get closer to him. I tried to struggle through the crowd but it was just hopeless. I began to get the feeling that if only I could get to him I would be healed. I made one last determined effort but it was no use at all. No matter how hard I strove I was not going to reach him. It was then that I felt compelled to stop struggling and to kneel down instead. I did so. In a moment Jesus was there, looking down at me. 'Why do you keep on struggling to get to me?' he asked. 'It would be so much easier for you just to let me come to you!' It was then that I realised just how much I *had* been struggling, with all my earnest, pleading prayers, trying to achieve salvation through hard work! The whole of my life was geared to this struggle to get to Jesus and it had reached its climax here in hospital. This message was to change my whole attitude to life and to ministry. It was a healing and a first step towards wholeness.

On the Friday I was encouraged at being the first one called to the operating theatre. No time for nerves! However, I had hardly left the ward on the trolly before I was called back; the specialist had not yet arrived. Each time the trolly entered the ward that day, I hoped that I would be the next but in the end it turned out that I was to be the last. I was all right until about mid-day but then, as the afternoon wore on, fear began to get a firm hold again. By the time the trolly came for me I was on edge, joking rather nervously with the porters and the theatre assistants. The 'pre-med' relaxed me and then I went off to sleep.

Jenny, my wife, had become concerned at the number of tests I had been having. She had begun to realise that there might be more to the problem than we had imagined. Shortly after 5 p.m. she phoned the ward to see if there was any news. I was back in bed, the gland had been successfully removed, but it had turned out to be malignant. That evening we were able to talk frankly about my illness and an appointment was made for us both to see the doctor who had performed the operation the next day. The news he gave us was not good. He had observed that the other glands were swollen and it seemed likely that the infection had begun to spread. A further operation would be necessary to remove many more glands and even then he could offer no great hopes that this would prevent the spread of the disease. We were both deeply shocked. I had never felt so downhearted in my life. It was not that I was frightened of dying, it was that I so much wanted to live. What would we tell the children, all our friends at St Mark's and my parents? For my father was himself dying of stomach cancer at the time! We decided to tell everyone the complete truth and to ask them all to pray.

It was a depressing few days that followed. Our faith was really under fire now. Where was God and what was he doing about all this? Why were we facing such an ordeal? What good could possibly come out of it? Jenny did some research into the nature of melanomas. It revealed the melanoma to be the most deadly of all the skin cancers; it was caused by the sun and it was usually fatal. We prayed that God would give us both the faith to cope.

After a few days the gloom began to lift. Jenny had gained great encouragement from part of Jim Glennon's book *Your Healing is Within You*. She began to see this as a real test of our faith in God. She also gained great inspiration from reading parts of the Bible and asked God to speak to her through it. She had been directed straight to the account of the healing of Naaman[1] and brought this encouragement to share with me. As I read through the story myself, I stumbled on the answer to my perpetual question as to why I could not be healed without all this surgery. Naaman had tried to dictate the manner and terms of his healing, but the only way he could be healed was to follow God's directions given through Elisha. I too had been trying to give God instructions as to how I wanted to be healed. The passage showed me clearly that this was not the way, that I must put myself entirely in the Lord's hands, without any conditions. By this time, too, I had decided that I was no longer prepared to accept passively the prospect of an early death. I would pray and fight to live. The gloom was beginning to lift. But there was another operation to face yet.

By now the nature of my illness had become generally known, and I shall never forget my gratitude for the wealth and extent of the support I received in prayer and care. Whilst the congregation was praying for both Jenny and myself we were also being given the kind of practical support that really lifted the strain upon the family. Anglican churches all over the diocese were praying for us, so were the local churches of other denominations. Our diocesan staff were praying for both myself and my father and the kind support of many clergy and others who came to see me was tremendous. I felt able to face the next operation with confidence that God was fully in charge.

However, as the Friday drew nearer I began to realise from little words that were said here and there that the operation was to be more extensive than I had thought. Fear began to get a grip once more. I became quite nervous and uneasy about it all and I asked that God would give me peace about the situation. That prayer was answered in two ways on the day before the operation. In the afternoon a young staff nurse began to speak of my operation with such matter-of-fact confidence that my worries began to ease. Then, in the evening, the ward chaplain brought me Communion and from that moment I knew peace. I even slept soundly through that night!

I was completely at peace throughout the next morning and shortly after mid-day I was taken down to the theatre. As I was wheeled in I passed another member of our congregation being wheeled out after her operation. I was to have the same specialist and he chuckled at the news that we both belonged to the same church. Many members of the congregation were at prayer for us both that day. Our church leaders had gathered in the vicarage and at the news that I had been taken down to the theatre they all went over to church to pray for me through the operation. I think it was the longest time of prayer that any had ever experienced for I was not back in the ward until 4.30 p.m.! I will never be able to express adequately my gratitude for this measure of prayer-support. All had apparently gone well, no further surgery was likely to be necessary, and all I had to do was to get better, which would probably take another fortnight in hospital and a further two weeks of convalescence. Things were beginning to look brighter.

A few days later I was visited by another doctor, this time from the area centre for the treatment of cancer. He wanted me to go over to Clatterbridge Hospital for radio-therapy treatment in about six weeks' time. I hesitated, for if, as I believed, I had been healed, surely this would not be necessary. But then, if I was putting myself completely in the Lord's hands I felt that I would have to go wherever he led me. I agreed to go.

Twelve days after the operation, the doctor came to see me. He brought two pieces of great news. First and most important, the glands which had been removed had now been carefully examined and all had been found to be clear; somehow the infection had not spread as expected. The second piece of good news was that I could get dressed and go home. Minutes later Jenny arrived. I couldn't wait to tell her the marvellous news, and what a prayer of thankfulness we shared together in the church as soon as we arrived home. It was wonderful to be able to look forward with real hope once again. God had done things in his own way but now I really could believe I had been healed.

In the meantime, our team Rector, Alan Treherne, and the diocesan staff had been busy making arrangements for me to go away for ten days of convalescence to a quiet corner of the diocese together with my family. How grateful we were for such a precious time together. Never before had we all appreciated each other so much!

Already I was beginning to see some of the good that was coming out of my experience. Through it I had gained a much deeper appreciation of the whole of life, so much that I had previously taken for granted: my life and health and strength, my family and all our friends at St Mark's. I knew that in the future I would always recognise every new day as the wonderful gift from God that it is. In my spiritual life I had come to learn what true submission to God's will involves, something *I* could only have learned through the experience of *having* to depend entirely on him. I had seen and experienced for myself how concerted prayer really can move mountains and had come to realise that even though we can sometimes wonder whether God has forgotten us, he is always by our side. Jenny too had grown tremendously in faith during this time. And then I had gained so much from the experience of being a hospital patient. Although I must have visited hundreds of people in hospital at different times I had never really understood what it felt like to be a patient – facing an operation, facing an unknown future, facing death. Now I have learned just what it feels like on the other side, and my hospital visits will never be quite the same again. Looking back over my time in Broadgreen Hospital, I have to say that apart from the operations and all the accompanying concerns, life in a hospital ward can actually be quite pleasant – especially when you know you're on the road to recovery.

It had been a tough month, but it ended on a good note. We had a wonderful ten days together as a family and we were able to return to St Mark's for a very moving Holy Week and Easter together. In Liverpool there is a familiar saying amongst older folk in times of trial or joy. They say: 'God's good!' That Easter, we too were truly able to say and to feel: 'God's good!'

At the beginning of May I was to go over to Clatterbridge Hospital for four weeks of radio-therapy treatment. I had been warned that although the treatment itself was quite painless, I would suffer a great deal of blistering and burning to the area that was to be treated – the right side of my chest and back. Nonetheless I was not unduly concerned for I felt that the worst was now past and anyway, I knew now that God was in charge.

It was when I was packing my case on the evening before I was to be admitted that I decided to look at my Bible reading for the next morning. This was what I read:

Israel, the Lord who created you says,
'Do not be afraid – I will save you.
I have called you by name – you are mine.
When you pass through deep waters, I will be with you;
your troubles will not overwhelm you.
When you pass through fire, you will not be burnt;
the hard trials that come will not hurt you.
For I am the Lord your God,
the holy God of Israel, who saves you' (Isa. 43:1-3 GNB).

I really felt elated. In the future this passage was to become something of a rock to my faith, and in so many ways it was to come true.

Clatterbridge turned out to be more like a hotel than a hospital. During the day we would wear our day-clothes and once we had received our treatment for the day we were free to ask permission to go out and about as we wished. It was during this time at Clatterbridge that I was able to begin the research for this book, in the peaceful atmosphere of the ward, and then I enjoyed so many lovely afternoons rambling across the Wirral countryside. In spite of my tender skin, I suffered no ill effects from the treatment; none of the severe blistering and no sickness. Even the common post-radio-therapy depression did not materialise, though I did experience an aversion to constant noise and became a little short-tempered with the children when they were at their noisiest. These four weeks at Clatterbridge turned out to be more like a retreat/holiday and within a week I was back at work again in the parish. All that remained were the regular check-ups – or so I thought.

On my next visit to the clinic the specialist suggested I should now undergo a course of chemo-therapy treatment. This was a real blow. I had thought that the treatment was all over. I had already seen something of the effects of these drugs on other patients; extreme sickness for hours on end, complete loss of hair, and then the injections! I had always been a coward as far as needles were concerned and the thought of daily injections into my veins repulsed me. 'Should I go or not?' I asked myself. After all, if I was now healed then chemo-therapy treatment was not necessary. But then, as I thought again of that passage from the words of Isaiah, somehow I knew that God was directing me to go through with it. It was fear and not faith that was holding me back. I agreed to go ahead with the treatment. I was to have six courses, one every third week over a period of four months, and in-between courses I could return to parish work if I felt well enough. So it was that in July I returned to my old ward in Clatterbridge and the new treatment began. For both Jenny and me this step had caused a slight knock to our faith and confidence in my healing. Quite unknown to me Jenny then asked God for another sign of confirmation that I had indeed been healed. If I had known what she was asking, I would have suggested she was asking the almost-impossible, for she asked that I should not lose my hair!

I will never forget the Monday that the treatment began. The injection itself was not so bad after all and afterwards I was sitting happily watching television – England playing in the World Cup – and thinking of my family and friends at St Mark's who were spending the evening together on a river cruise on the Mersey, an event I had thoroughly enjoyed myself in years past. And then the sickness started . . . It seemed bad at the time but the next day I was not too worried about the second dose. And so the treatment began. It was not at all pleasant, but not quite as bad as I had imagined, though each time I had to return to the hospital a horrible sinking feeling would begin a few days beforehand.

The sickness seemed to get worse day by day. During the third week I became more sick than usual and by the Wednesday I was becoming dizzy and light-headed, probably due to anxiety. On the Wednesday night I resolved to finish with the treatment altogether; I felt I couldn't take any more. That night I prayed to God to confirm that I was making the right decision. By next morning he had sorted me out and helped me to see things more clearly. It was true that I was not well enough to take any more treatment that week but there was really no reason why I should not come back to take the fourth course in two weeks' time. I was surprised that the doctors so readily agreed to this. They also promised to review the whole situation then, and I felt so relieved. Perhaps when I returned they would decide that I had had sufficient treatment anyway. I was 'signed off' work for a month, and during the two weeks' interval I was well enough for us all to take a holiday with relatives in the south of England.

We enjoyed another wonderful fortnight together. I became stronger and felt so much better. By the time I returned to Clatterbridge I had somehow convinced myself that the doctors would tell me that no further treatment would be necessary. When I arrived on the Monday morning they seemed surprised to see me back and my hopes lifted. I think they had imagined I wouldn't return again. After a brief consultation they suggested that the treatment should continue, but that I should receive additional drugs – tranquillisers – to help me cope with it. I was so bitterly disappointed that I was near to tears. But I agreed to go on with the treatment for as long as I felt I could.

As things turned out the tranquillisers did the trick and I found the latter three courses quite bearable. I slept a lot, time seemed to pass quickly, and neither injections nor sickness seemed so severe. I am told that I would walk about as if I was drunk and my memory was also affected; I could not recall the events of these weeks without prompting. One of the more amusing effects of this was that I could never remember who had been in to see me – it was very difficult at the time to sort out my vivid dreams from reality – and sometimes I would have to check with astonished friends whether they had actually come in to see me or whether I had dreamed it! Jenny would take me out in the car each evening, but I could remember little of what we did or where we went without being reminded. Some of my opportunist friends began to remind me of money I had borrowed from them at the time! The days passed quickly and in no time at all it was October and I had completed the treatment. Another week's holiday in the Lake District was our family celebration. At last it was all over and I could get back to normal life and work without the constant interruptions of hospital treatment. Now all that I had to do was to 'walk out my healing' in the way I had advised so many others in the past.

At first it was hard to simply brush aside all doubts and challenges, but day by day it has become easier as faith has grown. I begin every day by thanking God – from my heart – for my healing, and I use every opportunity that comes my way to affirm it as I talk to others. Like all who have had cancer, at every new ache or pain I ask myself, 'Could it be coming back?' But then I quickly dismiss such thoughts and thank the Lord again that I am healed. God has heard and responded in love to all our prayers and I have seen that message from Isaiah actually coming true as the year has gone by. I'm sure I will cling to those words for the rest of my life. And then, if I still need final assurance, I remember that almost-impossible sign that Jenny asked for. Although the chemo-therapy treatment had made me very ill at times, I did not lose my hair!

I have begun by writing of these experiences in the hope that they will help and encourage others as they have helped and encouraged me. I have experienced at first hand the ongoing battle between faith and fear. Fear causes doubt and worry, deep concern at the seriousness of the situation as a person is made to focus on himself and his troubles. Faith, on the other hand, calls us simply to focus on the Father, on his great love and mighty power, and to trust in him alone. I have come to realise that if we are to ask God to heal, then we must ask unconditionally, leaving the method, timing and nature of the healing in his hands. It is only when we can hand over the whole of our troubles to God and truly say, 'Your will be done,' that he can really take over. These are some of the deepest lessons I have learned.

We had also prayed, with laying on of hands, that my father too would be healed of the stomach cancer from which he had been suffering. During my early weeks in Clatterbridge he died. I believe that that was his healing. It must have been a terrible ordeal for my mother, to have both husband and son with cancer at the same time. But the Lord looked after us all, for Clatterbridge is only a few miles from my parents' home and I saw much more of them than I could have done otherwise. Had I not been in hospital at the time, I would not have been able to go out to see Dad on the day that he died, very peacefully, and Jenny and I would not have been so close at hand when Mum most needed us. Even in this we could see God's caring hands at work.

Through my illness I have been able to learn about God's healing power from the other side, as a patient. Many of the thoughts I am able to share with you through these pages have been deeply coloured by these experiences.

At St Mark's we have grown in faith as a church. At first some were asking, 'Why on earth doesn't God protect his people (and our Vicar) from such dreadful things as cancer?' Now we are able to affirm together that God can counter and conquer even cancer if we come to him faithfully in prayer. Together we have seen too how God can use such things to bring about greater good and fulfil his own purposes, enabling us to grow in faith at the same time.

I walk about today as a living witness to God's healing power through prayer. I will always be deeply indebted to our family at St Mark's and indeed to people throughout the diocese and even further afield for the prayers that have made me whole again. I will always be grateful to the doctors and surgeons who treated me with such care and skill. But above all I will always be most deeply thankful to our loving heavenly Father; that I am alive today, that I am privileged to be able to serve him and that I am the wiser for my experiences.

'To him be the glory, for ever and ever. Amen.'

Notes

1. 2 Kings 5: 1–15

Chapter 2

ASH WEDNESDAY

A Day of Prayer

It is now nearly half past seven on a damp and chilly Ash Wednesday morning. The doors of the little church are already open and in ones and twos a small number of men and women approach and enter to meet together to begin the day in prayer, for today has been designated a day of prayer at St Mark's.

The church is situated in the midst of one of many large housing estates on the outskirts of Liverpool. Like so many others, it can never be left open unattended. However, every six weeks or so – usually on a Wednesday – a day of prayer is called. Then the church does remain open all day, manned by the two full-time ministers and some of the church leaders, to build up to an evening service of prayer and praise with some special theme or purpose. Today the theme is one of prayer for healing, and so it is that the church leaders and ministers have come to begin the day together in prayer, especially prayer that the healing hands of God will be much in evidence during the course of the day to bring care, hope and healing to all who come openly and expectantly to receive from a loving heavenly Father.

After about half an hour the little group disperses again, some to go off to work, others to return home, but all to use the day as a day of prayer wherever they may be. Some are also fasting for twenty-four hours. During the day about two dozen people will call in at the church for moments of quietness and prayer and maybe too for a chat with someone about some pressing concern. Some of them have kindly allowed me to share with you a little of their lives.

One of the early visitors I will call Janet. She has been coming along to Sunday services for some weeks now, but has often been upset. Before today she had felt unable to share the reasons for her sadness. But as we chat together this morning she is able to share the secret she has been bearing alone since Christmas: at home her husband lies seriously ill and in great discomfort. The doctors have diagnosed an advanced cancer and do not expect him to live for longer than a few months. We pray together for his healing and that Janet may have the strength and courage to care for him during his illness.

Amongst the other morning visitors are Catherine, whose husband is recovering at home after a major operation, Brenda, who comes in preparation for tonight's service of prayer for healing, Alice, who has now recovered after a major operation just a year ago, Michelle, who comes to pray for her friend who is ill and feeling quite depressed at present, and John, our window-cleaner, who is a committed Roman Catholic and often stops by for a few moments of prayer in St Mark's.

Soon some of the church leaders return. Shortly afterwards Esther is brought by car. She is unable to venture out in the evenings, so she has arranged to come now so that we might pray with her for her healing. Her troubles began a year ago when, after surgery, a blood clot caused permanent damage to the nerves in her legs. Since then she has suffered considerable pain and felt very much at the end of her tether and desperate for help. Her first acupuncture treatment some weeks ago had brought a little relief, but no real healing. She was still unable to get about on her own and was always dragging her leg uncomfortably. It has been many months since she felt well enough to come along on a Sunday, but today she has prayerfully and determinedly prepared to come and seek God's healing. After a little chat and a prayer together, the church leaders quietly gather around and together we gently lay hands on her head and pray for her complete healing, in the name of Jesus Christ. We thank God for his loving touch, Esther weeps a little and then she is helped back to the car to be driven home.

The afternoon sees many more visitors: Jennifer, who last Ash Wednesday was, most incredibly, healed of the terrible, disabling effects of a motor-cycle accident forty years earlier; Isobel, who has suffered since childhood from a nervous disorder causing frequent fits and times of depression, but is now showing some signs of improvement; Mavis, who still has times of loneliness and depression since the death of her husband two years ago, but who battles on mârvellously and cheerfully and is always keen to play her full part in everything; and then come Marie and Heather, both of whom have often come to pray for healing for others, but this evening Marie has been encouraged to ask for healing for herself.

And so throughout the day people come and go, for many and varied reasons, most of them to return later for the evening service of praise and prayer for healing.

A Service of Prayer for Healing

It is now half past six and about thirty people have gathered in the church for a service of Holy Communion. The service is short but unhurried, quiet and devotional. Afterwards the church leaders move into a small room for further prayers and preparation together for the service that is to follow. By half past seven about fifty people are present. Most are members of St Mark's, one or two have come from other churches and some are here for the first time. Quite a number have been preparing carefully for coming forward this evening, some through prayer and fasting, others with a little counselling too, and a sense of hope and expectancy is evident.

Yet the service, though pleasant and worshipful, does not itself seem particularly special in any way. The many hymns are moving and well known and the readings, familiar to many, are words of encouragement from Isaiah and Luke for any who find their lives dominated by hurts and depressions. The simple address takes up that theme to show more clearly the various ways in which men and women can find themselves imprisoned by their circumstances and to show how Jesus longs to and can set them free. A young member of the choir sings a very moving song of hope before the congregation is led into a meditation of prayer for healing known as the 'Ring of Peace'.[1] As a distinct sense of peace settles upon the service, two quiet hymns sensitively lead up to the climax.

Members of the congregation who wish to are then invited to come forward to the communion rail for prayers with the laying on of hands. It is made clear that they may come forward for any genuine reason at all: for any kind of healing, great or small; for healing on behalf of someone else; as an act of thanksgiving for a healing; to make a personal commitment; as an act of prayer-commitment for a particular concern; or even to ask to be filled with the power of God's Holy Spirit. Men, women and children begin to come forward, much as they might at a Communion service, and each in turn is surrounded by a group of three church leaders and one of the ministers for prayer with laying on of hands. Some want to mention why they have come, others just kneel in silence. Some return to their seats with tears in their eyes, others with radiance on their faces, but most just as quietly as they came. Nearly everyone seems to have come forward for some reason or other, including children from the choir. It is clearly a familiar and accepted part of the church's life, for no one shows any sign of awkwardness or embarrassment.

A time of quietness follows, leading carefully into songs, hymns and prayers of praise and thankfulness. And so the service draws to its close just as gently as it began. Some of the congregation drift quietly home, others want to stay behind for a while for a cuppa and a chat.

Afterwards there seem to be very mixed feelings about the service. While some have experienced a deep sense of the presence of God throughout, others felt decidedly restless and uneasy, and a few have been quite unable to come

forward for prayers though they had previously intended to.
My own feelings were not very positive at all, but then they
had been coloured by the fact that I had a sore throat and was
suffering from a partial loss of voice which had not apparently improved in any way by the end of the service! And
then two of the ladies mention that they feel rather 'giggly'
and they cannot understand why!

For most I think it has been a helpful and moving service,
although on many previous occasions we have experienced a
far greater sense of prayer and praise. Yet we have been very
conscious of the Father's healing presence amongst us today
and in the days to come we shall, no doubt, become aware of
some of the ways in which he has been moving in our midst.

In the Days that Follow

In the remaining part of this chapter I would like to share
with you some of the experiences of those who came along on
Ash Wednesday. Each has kindly allowed this in the hope
that these experiences will offer some encouragement to
others to share in some way in the ministry of Christian
healing.

First of all let us return to Janet and Esther, who came
during the daytime. We had prayed that Janet's husband
might be healed. Just five days later he died peacefully in her
arms. She was heartbroken. However, after a time we were
able to thank God that he had so gently taken her husband
away from his terrible illness. Today Janet is just beginning
to be able to look forward a little and I believe that she has
found a new understanding of God's love through her painful
ordeals.

Esther recounts an unusual tale of her Ash Wednesday
experience:

As I came into the church that afternoon, it seemed as if
someone had waved a magic wand over everywhere; it was
different, beautiful and very peaceful. During the prayers I
felt that I wanted to cry all the time. As I got up to go, I

seemed to be able to walk more easily and I wasn't so short of breath as I usually am. Afterwards, when I got home, I felt that I had been somewhere really special.

For a time Esther felt better, looked better and found that she continued to get about with much more ease than previously. But sadly the improvement turned out to be short-lived. A few weeks later she visited the hospital for her second acupuncture treatment and this turned out to be very painful and quite unlike the previous visit. However, since then she has had further acupuncture treatment and is now able to move about more freely and we pray that her healing may soon be complete.

We move on now to hear of just a few of those who came forward at the evening service. I had been visiting Mary for some weeks before she came along on Ash Wednesday. She seemed rather a sad figure, completely trapped by the memories of two bereavements, the last one being seven years earlier. Although leading an active and outgoing life and giving the appearance of being assured and contented, deep down inside she felt lonely and depressed, often finding herself breaking into tears when she looked back over memories of earlier days of sunshine and happiness. At the service Mary too had felt restless and as if she wanted to get away from the church altogether. But at the invitation to come forward she was the first on her feet. She recounts: 'Everything seemed to stop at that moment, as I went forward and knelt down. I don't remember much else except that after the prayer, as you offered me your hand and I seized it, it didn't seem like your hand at all – it seemed like another hand, and I really felt that I belonged.'

I remember giving Mary a little hug as she left the church. Later she told me that once again it seemed like the hug of someone else!

Since then Mary's depression has begun to lift. She feels much more enthusiastic about her life and not nearly so lonely. She still has her tearful moments when thinking back over past memories, but the difference seems to be that they no longer imprison her as they had previously. The signs of strain seem to be lifting too as Mary endeavours to live in the present and make up for her years of gloom.

Linda is one of our teenage members. She came forward at the service with her father to ask for healing for his sister (Linda's aunt) who had been diagnosed as having a terminal cancer. In the days that followed she seemed to pick up considerably and felt much better in herself. But her weight loss and difficulty in eating continued and before long she was very sick again, with no signs that any physical healing had taken place. She has since died.

Stella is another of St Mark's teenagers. She has a pretty tough time at home, as her widowed mother is an invalid and Stella has to bear the weight of all the domestic responsibilities. For a girl of sixteen this inevitably becomes a great pressure on her time, energy and natural growing-up, and much support is bound to be needed. It seems sad that lately Stella has become much less aware of God in her life and has drifted away from many of her formerly close friendships in the church. On Ash Wednesday she came bearing many burdens – domestic, financial and social – together with the pressure of school-work and approaching exams, and the anxiety of just trying to cope with them all although still only a teenager. On the night, Stella recounts, she became very much caught up in the atmosphere of the service, and rather emotional. She left feeling easier and happier; her burdens and responsibilities no longer seemed so overpowering. Since then she has felt much calmer and more contented with life and seems to be coping more easily and not 'exploding' so often. Now and again things still get on top of her and she becomes depressed for a little while, but she is struggling to build up and depend upon her faith once again.

Richard had been a keen and lively member of St Mark's for some time. However, he felt bothered that his Christian life and service was not being lived out with the best of motives. The considerable number of responsibilities that he had taken up were being carried out much more out of a sense of moral duty than as real Christian service through his love of God. He believed that he should be giving more of himself, and came forward to make a new act of commitment. Since Ash Wednesday he has felt more inspired to give more fully of himself in his everyday life and service.

For Edna the service brought yet another in a long line of prayers for her healing. She suffers from Parkinson's disease and always looks incredibly lonely, lost and sad. Her husband died some years ago but she has a large, caring family who have been very good to her. I have spent many hours talking with her and we have prayed for her healing many times, yet she remains just the same. Edna's life seems filled with sadness and depression. She has guilty regrets about almost everything she does, and these feelings seem to rub off on to all who try to help her so that *they* begin to feel guilty and depressed too! Her Puritan type of approach to her faith leads her to preach at others – her family in particular. Many would-be helpers therefore soon choose to distance themselves from her, thus increasing her loneliness and isolation. After the Ash Wednesday service, Edna's condition began to deteriorate and the disease appeared to be affecting her mind too, so that she could not be left on her own. However, following a great deal of patient care from her family, she is now looking much better and is able to look after herself once more. Whilst she has not yet been completely healed, she really is so much better and her shaking is not nearly so prominent.

It was a year ago that Jennifer herself was healed, but now she was more concerned about her old friend Beryl. Some weeks earlier, Beryl had come to visit Jennifer. They had not seen each other for some time and both were rather shocked to find such changes in health in each other. While the previously disabled Jennifer could now walk comfortably again, the once-healthy Beryl was now crippled with arthritis and had a great struggle to get out of the car and up the stairs to Jennifer's flat. For the past month she had hardly been able to move and was now unable to go out without someone to help her. On hearing of Jennifer's healing she was soon keen to come along to the Ash Wednesday service herself.

However, on the night she found herself too ill to make it. So it was that – quite unknown to Beryl – Jennifer decided to come to the service not for her own needs, but in the hope that through her prayers and through receiving the laying on of hands and prayer God would touch and heal her friend. Within a few days Beryl's arthritis had completely disappeared, much to the astonishment of her doctor, and it has not returned since. What a joy it was for Jennifer when her friend told her she was better – and they both realised why!

For Sarah it was now well over three years since she had been disabled by a stroke. As a result she has been unable to get about without the aid of a wheel-chair and feels considerable frustration at her loss of speech and inability to put together her sentences. She too has received prayer with laying on of hands on many occasions, but progress has been painfully slow, though there is no doubt that she is considerably better than she was three years ago. Since the service there has been improvement in her speech, which suddenly returned to near-normality, but she is still unable to get about unaided. I believe it will take a great deal of determination on her part, and persistent commitment in prayer on ours, for her to be healed completely.

Finally there was Barbara, whose husband had died suddenly four months earlier through a stroke, leaving her a heartbroken widow with a nine-year-old son. The past four months had been a time of awful agony for her, as she hopelessly tried to fight back her tears day after day. She struggled on with her lonely tasks as a housewife and a mother, but inwardly she felt she was going nowhere. Her young son Alan had been a tremendous support to her, and seemed to have coped so well, but Barbara could see no way out of her misery and could only wistfully reflect on the happiness of days gone by. I had been to see her a number of times before the service. It was clear that her faith in God was deep, but she was angry with him, confused and wondered if the events were some kind of divine judgement or punishment. Eventually she had been able to accept that this was not so and that God really did love her, but still she felt desperately let down by all that had happened. She just couldn't bring herself to look forward again, she couldn't accept her husband's death and she couldn't stop crying.

Barbara came to the Ash Wednesday service with her hopes high. She cried her way through the service, felt very embarrassed about it and didn't enjoy the experience at all. It had been good to see young Alan singing his heart out, and she was grateful that another member of the congregation came across to comfort her. She was able to come forward as planned, but she went home feeling deeply disappointed and more upset than ever. However, in the days that followed she decided to 'claim her healing'. Every morning, and often again during the day, she would thank God for healing her, even though she felt rather hypocritical because she didn't seem to be any better at all. Yet she persevered. After about a month she realised that she was beginning to get through the days more easily and without becoming so upset. She was even able to begin to look forward a little and to actually enjoy doing one or two things again. All of her wonderful memories were still very much with her, but no longer did they seem to be holding her in the past.

When I called on Barbara a few weeks ago we both accepted that the healing she had been thanking God for was now much in evidence. As we knelt down together to thank God for her healing, I laid hands on her just once more, in thanksgiving, and she experienced the warmth and the power of the Holy Spirit that so often comes at such a moment. When she lifted up her head she smiled, and what a beautiful and radiant smile it was – the smile of someone who has been touched and healed by Jesus Christ himself.

Notes

1. The 'Ring of Peace' is a method of healing prayer, presented by Roy Lawrence in his book *Invitation to Healing* (see appendix 2). It is a form of meditation which enables participants to experience the presence and peace of Christ.

Chapter 3

HOW IT ALL BEGAN

My Own Background

After my ordination into the Anglican Church, the first five years of my ministry were spent as a curate in the parish of St Mary, West Derby, also in the Diocese of Liverpool. These were very happy years for me and were to stand me in good stead for future responsibilities as a vicar. I soon found that much of my time involved visiting those who were ill – some seriously or even dying. It was when I was with those who were suffering from the most serious complaints that I would feel the most helpless and inadequate. Words of comfort and reassurance can feel very hollow when you both realise the seriousness of a situation. We would pray that they would soon be better, that pain might ease and that God would look after them, but all too often my part of the prayer was tempered by my thoughts about the likely outcome. Because I really had no concept of my prayers being likely to alter the course of events, they were timid and ineffectual.

The most traumatic experience for me during this period concerned the illness of a young teenage boy whom I shall call Simon. The development of a bone cancer resulted in the amputation of one of his legs in the hope that this would prevent its spreading to other parts of his body. Simon's family were all members of St Mary's, and while there was this hope we all prayed in earnest that he would be all right. However, the operation had not prevented its spreading and soon Simon was back in hospital again. Still we all prayed that he would be healed. I prayed more earnestly and committedly for Simon's healing than I had ever prayed for anyone before. Yet in my heart of hearts I believed that there was little hope that he would ever recover. I could not see how God could heal him now. Soon those prayers changed to focus more upon relief from his sufferings, that he might soon be taken on into the new life, and for comfort and support for his family.

His family certainly felt that support – but then we believed that they would! But Simon died, as we had anticipated. Afterwards I found myself with many unanswered questions about the nature of God and the effectiveness of prayer. At the time I had seen my role as being one of bringing comfort and support to Simon and his family. But then I had no real concept of being in any position to bring in God's healing power.

Tentative First Steps

When I arrived at St Mark's in 1976 the church had only been open for two years. It was one of three churches in the newly-formed Gateacre Team Ministry. Everyone seemed to be looking forward with great hope and expectancy, and I was able to throw myself into the ministry with much zest and enjoyment. I began to plan and arrange the ministry of the church in a thorough and comprehensive way, as I had been trained to, with much concern for the major problems in our community. Things began to move along quite encouragingly and a really exciting vision for the future began to emerge. But it was *my* vision – and God had other plans in mind!

Once more my pastoral ministry involved visiting the sick, the suffering and the dying, and in Childwall Valley there seemed to be even more sickness about. Again I would often feel the frustrations of being resigned to the presence of so much sickness and not having the gifts or skills to be of any really worthwhile help. I became curious about little snippets of news about ways in which the ministry of healing was beginning to develop through the Church. I wanted to know more.

By this time I had been joined at St Mark's by a deaconess, Ann Barnett, who already had a little experience of this ministry, and together we began to study and pray for guidance as to what we should do. It was Francis MacNutt's book *Healing* (see appendix 2) which had the most positive and direct influence on our thinking during this time.

Soon we felt it right to take our first careful steps and we asked Ruth, a member of St Mark's congregation, if she would like us to pray and to lay hands on her to ask God to heal her. She suffered from arteriosclerosis of the head and shoulders, a form of hardening of the arteries which brought on periods of depression and inability to think straight. Since having a number of heart-attacks, she was forced to take things very easily whenever one of these periods of depression came on, and to stay at home and away from everything until it was over.

Ruth accepted our offer gratefully and we duly prepared in prayer and in method. In due course Ann and myself arrived at her home, and shared together in a little service of prayer for her healing. As we laid hands upon her, I remember feeling a distinct sense of tingling in my hands and arms, and later on Ruth told us that she had experienced a feeling of warmth as we prayed for her. I firmly believed that we were going to see her healed as a result of our visit and our prayers – but I was wrong. We continued to pray for her, but no improvement was apparent and soon it became clear that she had not been healed, that she was no better at all.

We were deeply disappointed. I was particularly concerned in case Ruth's faith had been harmed in any way through it all. But Ruth accepted her disappointment with great courage. What were we to do now? In view of this first apparent failure, I felt it best that we ventured no further in this kind of ministry until we understood more and had some direct guidance from God that this was what he wanted us to be doing.

Forced to Prayer

In the meantime other aspects of the ministry were occupying a great deal of our time and attention, particularly the prevalence of 'evil presences' affecting people and homes in the local area. We had to seek a great deal of advice and support in how to respond to these problems, and were wisely advised not to proceed on our own. So Ann and I gathered around us a really committed little group of members of St Mark's who agreed to support us in prayer as we responded to each of these particular problems.

Soon our meetings became quite regular and we were encouraged by the ways in which we were seeing our prayers being answered and God's power at work. We began to pray for people in all kinds of needs and troubles, including the sick. At last we were beginning to experience and realise the power and effect of committed prayer in our life together.

A number of parishioners came to be very much in our prayers at this time. In particular Susan, a little girl who had recently had a leg amputated because of a bone cancer. Her family and doctors were waiting anxiously to see whether this would stop the spread of the cancer. For me this brought back memories of Simon and I dreaded the thought of going through the experience again with Susan and her family. So it was that we held our first day of prayer at St Mark's, a day of prayer for healing, culminating in an evening service of prayer for healing at which we prayed by name for Susan and also others who had been much in our thoughts. It was a moving service. No personal ministry of laying on of hands was involved at this stage, but we prayed for each in love and care to ask for their healing. Although we saw no striking effects through the service, we felt encouraged to move onward.

Ann was very keen for us to develop a permanent ministry of prayer for healing with laying on of hands, but I felt cautious as a result of our experiences to date. I believed that we should not move on in this way without some direct guidance from God that this was what he wanted us to do. So we decided to ask for a sign. We asked that without any prompting from us, someone would come forward to ask for this ministry.

A 'Green Light' At Last

Don described himself as a casual churchgoer. When his wife began to come along to St Mark's quite regularly, now and again Don would come with her. However, he was a born worrier. He worried about everything, and he seemed to have plenty to worry about, too. When he had been working, the pressures of the job had brought on a nervous breakdown. Now he had been unemployed for some time and had difficulty coping with the resultant frustrations. Besides this, he suffered a great deal of pain and discomfort from arthritis in his shoulder, neck and spine, which he treated with a fine collection of painkillers, tranquillisers and various other remedies. He did not appreciate being classed as disabled and regular bouts of depression and headaches made him irritable and bad-tempered at home and rather difficult to live with. Although he realised that he was putting his marriage under considerable strain, he felt quite powerless to do anything at all about the situation. When, finally, he was given a surgical collar and was told that he would have to wear it for the rest of his life, it seemed like the last straw.

It was during one of his times of depression and pain that Don decided he would prefer to spend his Sunday evening at home and let his wife go off to church on her own. He switched on the television instead, to watch the Sunday evening service. It turned out to be a service from St Stephen's Church in Prenton, Birkenhead, which involved prayers for healing with laying on of hands. During the service Roy Lawrence spoke about the experience of depression and about God's great power to heal. Don's instant response was, 'That's what I want!' The next day he saw Ann, told her excitedly about the service and asked where he could receive this ministry. And so it was that we responded by promising that *we* would offer prayers for his healing with the laying on of hands.

Now that we had our clear sign, we felt it important to proceed with much prayer and carefulness. We decided that the little service should be a part of our midweek fellowship meeting, and that it should involve everyone there. We asked the members of our prayer support group to take part in the laying on of hands, and we decided to anoint Don with oil at the same time (see chapter 11). I spent some time in helping Don to prepare himself for coming to the meeting, and about three weeks later he duly joined us at the fellowship group for the service.

Don came to the meeting alone. He hadn't realised that his wife could have come with him. He had never been to the fellowship group before, so he wasn't quite sure what to expect. Towards the end of the meeting Don was invited to come forward to kneel down on a cushion in the middle of the room. About eight people gathered around him and gently laid their hands on his head, while I anointed him with oil, and we all prayed for his healing. Although we only touched Don lightly, he explains:

Soon the pressure of the weight of hands on my head became almost unbearable. But then a lovely warm feeling began to spread everywhere, as if I was plugged in to very soothing electricity. I started to shake, first in my left arm and then all over. All my energy seemed to be draining away, and with it went my aches and worries. I felt all limp and lovely! In the distance I could hear singing, beautiful music, like a great choir singing the most moving songs I'd ever heard. It wasn't exactly words that they were singing, more like a humming, and then there was this marvellous orchestra with violins and things, just like Mantovani!

A tall shadow drew close to me, and his thin brown arms picked me up and held me to his chest. I just wanted to stay there forever and enjoy the wonderful peace. But the peace was interrupted by Neil's voice calling me to stand up. I felt so angry that he was spoiling it all, I could have thumped him!

When I was taken back to my seat I didn't really know

where I was. We sang a song or a hymn, but I kept rubbing my hands together all the time – I don't know why. When the meeting finished I was in such a hurry to go that I tried to put on the wrong coat. Then, as I rushed off home, I felt so excited that I wanted to shout out with happiness.

Don rushed out into the night before anyone had a chance to speak to him. He arrived home flushed and breathless. His eyes were sparkling and his speech was slurred. His wife was angry. He couldn't have been to the meeting after all – he must have been out drinking instead. For a while she refused to believe his protests, until he asked her to sit down for a game of chess. She was puzzled because although in the past they had often enjoyed games of chess together, more recently he just hadn't had the patience for it. As they enjoyed their game of chess together she realised that something had happened to her husband: he wasn't drunk, but he was different!

That night, in bed, Don was restless and burning. He couldn't sleep at first and was quite sick. But when he awoke the next morning he felt like a new man. All his worries had gone and he was full of health and happiness. Life seemed so much brighter and clearer, like the first sunny day of spring-time. When he went out everyone seemed to be smiling and, although he usually preferred to keep himself to himself, today he wanted to talk to everyone. Even the buildings seemed clearer and better defined. Don knew he was really living again.

I had not heard anything of Don's adventures and it was with some hesitancy that I knocked at his door two days later to see if he was any better. I wanted to apologise for letting him rush off home without a word after the fellowship meeting. However, I didn't get the chance, for Don was so eager to tell me his tale of how he had been healed.

Since then Don has repeated his story many times and to hundreds of people. No longer is he depressive and irritable. No longer is he frustrated at not having employment – he spends so much of his time visiting others and working on the church grounds and gardens that he wouldn't have the time to go out to work now anyway! Don's arthritis is not completely healed and he is still classed as being disabled, but most of the tablets and medicines have long-since disappeared. He has long periods of remission – especially when he is at his busiest – and his marriage has really begun again!

Soon everyone was talking about the new Don. We were not used to seeing people's personalities change overnight. Further requests for prayers for healing soon followed and this ministry became a regular part of our weekly fellowship meetings, with quite a number of healings taking place.

One who came was little Susan. She had not been healed and her cancer was spreading. The doctors held out little hope for her. She too was anointed, and we prayed with all our hearts that Susan would be healed. I really believed that she would be, but shortly afterwards Susan died. She had a difficult time, but it could have been much worse. We were all deeply hurt and did the best we could to offer comfort and support to her parents. We wondered where this left our ministry of healing until we were shown in a rather wonderful way that our prayers *had* been answered; Susan *had* been healed, in that sometimes God has to take the person from the illness instead of the illness from the person. This was still very hard to accept because we loved Susan and her parents very much. But once we really knew that she was indeed healed and in the Father's loving care, then our ministry of prayer for healing was able to continue.

Moving Onward

It soon became clear to us that this part of our ministry should not and could not be confined to midweek fellowship meetings in a cosy but rather special room in the church hall. It also seemed necessary and right to be clear about who should be formally sharing in this ministry. After much prayer it was agreed that we should call another day of prayer on Ash Wednesday 1980, and that the climax to that day should be a great service of praise and prayer for healing with laying on of hands. At the service those who were to take a greater share in the pastoral overseeing of the church – including the healing ministry – would be commissioned.

In the days leading up to it, we talked with all who had been involved in our little prayer support group, and with other church members too, about how we would develop a shared pastoral ministry. We discussed who that ministry would be shared with and what commitments and responsibilities it would involve for everyone. As a result, eight members agreed to prepare to become church leaders by working closely with the full-time ministers to share in the pastoral oversight of the church, including the ministry of healing.

On Ash Wednesday, at the evening service, they were duly commissioned. It was a great day of prayer, praise and thanksgiving and turned out to be a milestone in our life and ministry at St Mark's. This was the first of many such services which were to see men, women and children from our own congregation, the local community and other churches in the diocese coming forward to receive healing from God. We have seen few instant healings; most have been gradual or after a little time; we have not seen a cripple throw away his crutches and leap for joy, or experienced the thrill of a blind man discovering he can see again. But we have seen many wonderful healings of all kinds, some of which you will be able to read of in the chapters that follow.

Ups and Downs

Since then we have experienced many ups and downs and I know that the full-time ministers would not have survived the many pressures without the loving and prayerful support of those church leaders and other members of the congregation. At first there were those who were concerned that we might be beginning to go overboard, that all kinds of unnecessary emotionalism were being brought into the church or that we were following some new radical and gimmicky trend. It took a long time to allay such fears, before people could see for themselves that God was indeed moving in a very powerful, but gentle and quiet way amongst us.

There were others who had shown concern about how church leaders had been chosen and about what authority they had. Again it has taken much time and patience to show that they were chosen to serve the congregation. Recently our church leaders have become church elders, developing their ministry in new and more demanding ways.

We have felt sadness and frustration when many of those who have come forward have not been healed. There have even been times when we have felt almost overtaken by the volume of sickness and suffering around us. Yet we have emerged from tunnels of darkness time and again into the glorious sunshine, and the various challenges and setbacks have been far outweighed by the joys and encouragements. We have really experienced the perfect tenderness of God's love and care for us; we have shared the deep joy of those who have been wonderfully healed by him; steadily we have begun to appreciate the greatness and power of God as he works among us; and we have learned to become more dependent upon his power and more sensitive to his guidance in our daily lives.

Today the healing ministry is no longer a controversial issue at St Mark's. All have been able to see that it is not sensational, over-emotional or embarrassing, but relevant, reverent and real. Prayer for healing with laying on of hands is now a familiar part of Sunday evening services, and members can ask for this ministry at any of our Communion services. Special services still take place, but now just four times a year. Two of these are on Wednesday evenings after a day of prayer, and two are on Sunday evenings.

There have been changes of ministers and church leaders, changes of approach and understanding, changes in faith and expectancy. Yet we are still in the very child-like stages of learning how to handle with great care a very precious and wonderful gift from God. And it is in this relationship with our loving heavenly Father that we move onward, in the confidence that he is lovingly and caringly opening up before us a road which we must try to keep to.

Chapter 4

THE HEALING HANDS OF GOD

'There is nothing in all creation that will ever be able to separate us from the love of God which is ours through Christ Jesus our Lord' (Romans 8:39 GNB).

1. What is God really like, and how does he regard sickness?

If we are to consider setting out along a road which calls for committed prayer to God for healing, then it is vital that first of all we make sure that we are clear about our relationship with God, what he is really like and how he regards sickness and suffering. Although we cannot entirely understand the ways of God – why some prayers are answered and others apparently not – we *are* given absolute proof of the extent of God's love for us, and plain evidence of his attitudes to illness.

Affirmations

i) God is a loving Father who wants the very best for his children.

Jesus continually encouraged his followers to look upon God as a child looks upon its loving father. We are called to pray to him as Father,[1] and to respond to his love as children.[2] All of us will remember something of what it is to be a child, to be dependent upon our parents for love and care, for food and

clothing, indeed for everything. Perhaps we can also remember with delight special moments of closeness to father
or mother.

Although I find it a struggle to give my three children all
the fatherly attention that they would like, now and again –
in turn – I love to take out each of them alone, for just a few
hours of undivided love and attention. We really treasure
these times together. I believe this is how God wants to be
with us.

On looking back to childhood days we might reflect that
our own parents had their human weaknesses. Perhaps we
felt that they were sometimes hard on us or a little unfair;
maybe they would say things that hurt us without realising;
they may have seemed impatient, bad-tempered or un-
reasonable at times; it may even have been that they could
never show us love, care and attention at times when we
really needed it. I am increasingly aware of my own shortcomings as a father, and no doubt those of you who are also
parents will be conscious of your own weaknesses and failings
in some ways. Nevertheless, you will know what it is to really
love your children. You will also appreciate how painful it is
to see them ill or suffering, how much you agonise when you
see them hurt in any way.

If this is how imperfect earthly parents feel towards their
children, how much more deeply will our perfect heavenly
Father agonise over the sickness, hardships or sufferings of
his children. There is a lovely passage in Matthew's Gospel
which highlights the love and care of God for his creation; the
birds, the flowers and ourselves.[3] If God has taken such
trouble about the welfare of birds or the beauty of flowers,
how much more is he bound to be concerned for the health
and happiness of his children.

I believe that the most helpful way in which we can relate
to God and begin to understand his ways is to regard him as
our perfect heavenly Father. Then we can begin to understand the extent of his love for us, the faithfulness of his care
for us and just how much each one of us really does mean to
him.

ii) The Father longs for each one of us to respond to his love as faithful children.

It follows now that – as our perfect loving Father – God must want the very best for each of his children. He will want us to be loving and faithful to him, to be good and obedient, and he must want us to grow up strong and healthy in every way – and to find real fulfilment and happiness in our adult lives.

As we grow, he will be happy if we are dependent upon him and come to him to share and find relief from all our little worries and problems. He will be glad to give us all that we really need because of our loving relationship with him.[4] But should we become spoiled or demanding children, then he is bound to be deeply hurt and unable to give us all that we might demand of him.

Nobody likes to see spoiled or demanding children throwing tantrums in a toyshop or being rude, nasty and thoughtless because the required sweets are not forthcoming. How sad it is to see a child who is always 'on the want', treating parents just as necessary providers, instead of responding to them in real love. And yet, how easy it is for us to slip into this kind of pattern in our prayer-relationship with God, to be always wanting, often thoughtless and even abusive when we don't get our way. How easily we can begin to treat God merely as our necessary provider, the 'genie of the lamp', without ever responding to him in thankful love.

What our Father longs for is children who love him, children who want to please him, who value above all else the family bond of dependence upon him and who – out of that loving relationship – will always come to him to share their needs, concerns and problems.

As Jesus taught us, so we pray: 'Our Father . . . may your will be done on earth as it is in heaven'.[5] But is it really God's will that is our greatest desire, or do we – like the spoiled child – really want to pray: 'my will be done . . .'? It is only when *our* will is truly a part of *God*'s will, when our relationship with the Father is such that we long to please him and to see his ways fulfilled, it is only then that we are responding to his love as faithful and obedient children, and it is only then that we can be sure that he is going to provide for all our needs.

Misunderstandings

i) The misconception that God sends sickness to punish or correct his wayward children.

'What have I done to deserve this?' asks the young man faced with the seriousness of his complaint. 'I've always tried to live a good life, and now this . . . !' moans the bereaved widow. While the man who has just lost his job wonders what he can do to get back in to God's favour.

In these and many other ways, misfortune or illness can come to be seen as some kind of divine punishment calling for repentance or retribution. Perhaps this idea of God's nature has been drawn from undeveloped Old Testament concepts of God as being separate and distant from his people, filled with anger at our unrighteousness and seeking to discipline his people by bringing suffering upon them.

Yet this type of picture of God is entirely superseded by the New Testament understanding of him as our heavenly Father, which Jesus gave us. Now, above all else, we can see him as the God of boundless love, of infinite patience, and we are offered this new relationship as God's children.[6]

We know only too well that all children are bound to have their moments of disobedience and failure, and there will be times when punishment is called for – perhaps a smack, a harsh word or the denial of some pleasure as a corrective for the future. But would any sane parent wish sickness or suffering upon any one of his children as a punishment or corrective, no matter what they had done? As an ordinary father, I just cannot believe it! Even less can I believe that our perfect loving heavenly Father would ever bring illness or agony upon any one of us as some sadistic act of retribution or reprisal – not the God of the New Testament!

Whilst it is clear that there are times when our own sinfulness can actually bring about illness,[7,8] it must be pointed out that this kind of sickness is the natural consequence of our own evil, and not some punishment from God. I find any idea of a heavenly Father who sends sickness and suffering to correct and punish his children quite inconceivable, totally repugnant and entirely out of step with the teaching and ministry of Christ. We must firmly dispel any ideas of sickness being sent from God to punish or correct.

ii) The misunderstanding that we should accept sickness as a cross that we are called to bear.

On various occasions Jesus warned his followers that they would have to endure many trials and tribulations. Great sufferings lay ahead for those who followed him faithfully, and each would need to be prepared to 'carry his cross'.[9] Many have wrongly equated this 'cross' with sickness, and taken Christ's words as a directive to accept pain and suffering through illness as being the way of Christ and the will of God.

In fact, on no occasion did Jesus ever even hint that this 'cross' involved illness of any kind. Quite the reverse: he opposed sickness constantly throughout his ministry and taught his followers to do the same. He did point out that this 'cross' would involve persecution, trials, beatings, betrayal and even death,[10] but not sickness.

It is therefore clear that illness and suffering are not to be accepted passively as being something that God wants us to bear for him. How could our loving Father ever gain pleasure or purpose from seeing his children patiently enduring sickness? Christ has already borne the real cross for us.

iii) The misconception that God doesn't care about me and my troubles.

'I wish God loved me and looked after me as he cares for you,' were the sad words of a lonely young woman. 'I've always been the odd one out and things never seem to go my way!' She had been the next-to-youngest of a large family, had many relationship problems and always seemed so sad. Her health was generally poor – a continuous tale of one minor illness after another.

It is quite surprising how many people have come to see themselves as the black sheep of God's family, as outcasts in whom the Father has little interest. They may go to great lengths to try to win his love and attention, and to earn the respect of others too, but they always seem to end up with a sense of failure and frustration. I believe this kind of outlook on life almost always stems from our own upbringing and early relationships with parents.

This highlights one danger in the idea of seeing God as Father, in that we might merely equate him with an earthly parent. This image would not be at all helpful to someone whose father was a drunken brute who eventually deserted the family to run off with another woman! And if our father (or mother) treated us as the odd one out as a child, then it is hardly surprising if we grow up feeling that God treats us in just the same way. It is really important therefore that we do not just see God as being like an earthly parent, but that we realise that he is the perfect Father – filled with love for each one of us. Just as God does not have favourites, so too he does not make outcasts. It is we who put ourselves in positions of either being able to receive God's favour or else being apart from him. A careful look at Luke, chapter 15, makes this very plain indeed.

Not only does God care for every one of us but, much more, he cares for every part of each of us. So often I hear people tell me that their complaint is far too trivial for God to be concerned about it. Just as a father is concerned about a splinter in his child's finger and will go to great lengths to remove it, so too God is concerned with every little worry of ours, no matter how tiny it may seem. We must take great care that we never set ourselves apart from God through believing that he doesn't care about our little troubles or that he doesn't love us any more.

There is a helpful little fable that brings out this point. It tells of a man whose life was hard with many periods of trouble and illness. When he died, and was able to look back over his life, he saw it in the form of footprints across a great stretch of sand. At first he was encouraged to see a second set of footprints beside his own, for he realised that they were the footprints of Christ. But then he was saddened to notice that at the toughest times of his life there was only one set of prints. 'Why did you desert me at the times when I most needed you?' he asked of Jesus. 'I would never desert you,' came the reply. 'Where you see only one set of footprints, I was carrying you!'

God's View of Sickness

i) Sickness is not a part of God's will for the world.

'Why is there sickness at all,' you might well ask, 'if it is not a part of God's will for the world?' It is very clear that our world is not as God would have it be. It is a fallen world. There are very many disturbing elements in our life, especially in our relationships with one another at all levels, which must bring great pain to the heart of our heavenly Father. Some of the prophets of the Old Testament were particularly sensitive to the sufferings of God. The Father longs for his people to be whole in every way, and that wholeness involves correct relationships, with him and with others, and healthiness in our everyday lives.

Just as the Father suffers to see his children's wholeness shattered by quarrels, bitterness and fighting, so too he suffers to see that wholeness replaced by ill-health. His will for our world is health and wholeness for all, but sadly we have not been prepared to accept his will for us all. Conflicts of all kinds are the result of this, and sickness too. Yet we can be encouraged that in his great love the Father has still given us much with which to fight against disease: the skill of doctors, the care of counsellors, the help of medicines and the power of prayer.

ii) God can use sickness to bring about good.

Although God does not send sickness upon anyone, it does seem that sometimes he can use it to bring about some good. I believe it is important we acknowledge that it is not uncommon for good things to come about as a result of illness.

There are many who would acknowledge that they have grown closer to God, or even come to faith, through their illness or the illness of someone else. Others have been brought to see the error of their ways through ill-health, while many more have only gained a true appreciation of the value of life and health as a result of their illness. It is frequently through sickness – at the point of healing – that we are able to really acknowledge the glory of God. There are examples of this in the healing ministry of Christ.[11]

In order to consider more fully God's view of sickness, we must look at the ministry of Jesus. It is in his character and from his reactions to sickness and suffering that we perceive most plainly the love and the will of God.

2. What is Jesus like, and how does he regard sickness?

In the character, life and ministry of Jesus we draw closest to seeing not only what God is like and his attitude to sickness, but also what he wants us to be like and how he wants us to react to sickness. Furthermore, it is through Christ, his life and power, his death and resurrection and his commission to heal,[12] that we can claim the right, as his Church, to bring healing today.

Many books and countless pages have been written about the person of Jesus and it is impossible to do justice to him within a few paragraphs. But I want to highlight some important characteristics, seen in his life and ministry, which are especially relevant to our theme. These are his love of the Father and devotion to his will, his faith in God's power and promises and his love for people and ways of caring for them.

What is Jesus really like?

i) His love of the Father and devotion to his will.
One of the hallmarks of Jesus' ministry is his closeness to God and absolute devotion to his will. Time and again we read in

the Gospels of Jesus going away on his own somewhere quiet for long periods, to be with his Father in prayer. In John's Gospel his closeness to God is clearly spelt out.[13]

It was through his oneness with God, maintained by prayer, that Jesus was able to perform such mighty works throughout his ministry. How often his greatest triumphs followed times of retreat for prayer! The crucial importance of this prayer-relationship with God is borne out by his words to the disciples as he healed the boy convulsed by a demon. The disciples had not been able to heal him: 'His disciples asked him privately, "Why couldn't we drive it out?" He replied, "This kind can come out only by prayer." '[14]

Jesus lived and died to reveal and fulfil the Father's will. It was a part of God's will that he should heal the sick,[15,16] and it is significant that so much of Christ's ministry was spent in doing just that! As his ministry developed he spoke more and more of the destiny that awaited him in order to carry out his Father's will, and it was by his closeness to God in prayer that he was able to carry it through.[17]

Just as prayer was the means by which Jesus was able to maintain his earthly ministry, so too prayer is the means by which we are called to continue his ministry today. Without closeness to the Father in prayer his healing power cannot be released. Unless we are prepared to make our prayer-relationship with God our 'life-line', then we need read no further.

ii) His faith in God's power and promises.

Arising from his closeness to the Father and knowledge of his will, Jesus was able to have absolute faith in God's power – not just for healing, but for everything. Much of Jesus' teaching was geared towards showing his followers how to really depend on God, in faith, for everything – material, physical or spiritual needs.[18] To reinforce this teaching he also assured us of the Father's promises to meet all the needs of his children.[19] These will be considered in more detail in chapter 7.

To read of Jesus' complete faith, or even of the marvellous

faith and works of great Christians, can be a great inspiration. On the other hand it can sometimes cause us to become
more conscious than ever of our own lack of faith. However, if
we can just take the first step of faith, by making ourselves
available for the power of Jesus to work in us and through us,
then our faith in God's power and promises will surely begin
to grow.

iii) His love for people and ways of caring for them.

Jesus healed the sick both to show that it was the Father's will
that he should, and also because he really loved people and
shared in God's pain at their sufferings. This is borne out
throughout his ministry in many different ways.

Time and again his compassion and pity for the people is
mentioned in the different Gospels. He always seemed to feel
great compassion when faced with the eager crowds,[20] and
some of his healings appear to have come solely out of his
compassion, rather than as the result of requests.[21] The
sensitive and careful way he had of healing the sick is
especially brought out in the accounts of the healings of the
deaf-mute[22] and of the blind man at Bethsaida.[23] Much of his
ministry was spent with those regarded as outcasts, but Jesus
was never willing to accept anyone as such; he was even
prepared to touch a leper in order to heal him.[24]

His love for people was such that he was willing to risk
defying the authorities on many occasions in order to heal.
He had no qualms at all about forgiving sins in order to heal[25]
or about healing on the Sabbath.[26] His healings were for the
benefit of the sick, and he refused to perform miracles as
spectacles for the benefit of the curious.[27]

Jesus loved people as individuals – like the rich young
man who had tried so hard to follow him but fell one huge
step short,[28] and together – like the beloved but unfaithful
people of Jerusalem.[29] Ultimately Christ's deep love for all
men has been established and proved in his willingness to
go to the cross for us. There can be no greater love than
this.[30]

It has been claimed justifiably that love is the most healing

force in the world. The greatest love that the world has ever
known is the love of God, in Christ. Undoubtedly, therefore,
the love of Christ is the greatest healing power of all.

If we are to continue Christ's healing ministry, then we too
must have a measure of his love for people. We need to be
willing to let Christ's healing love flow through us.

His Ministry to the Sick

i) His reactions to sickness and the sick.
Jesus' ministry was concerned with meeting people in their
various situations of need. Time and again Jesus was faced
with illness of all kinds. On every occasion he opposed it,
always and without fail he healed and he healed everyone
who came to him for healing. What a record!

Jesus regarded sickness as an enemy and opposed it with
authority. Everyone seemed to recognise the authority in his
teaching, his counselling, and when he healed people his
words always had that firm ring of authority.

He opposed sickness, yet he always showed great love and
care for the sick as we have already seen. If we are to follow
Christ's ministry we can be left in no doubt that we too must
oppose sickness and show great love and care for those who
are sick. Whilst we can never hope to match his success rate,
we must still do everything we can to bring Christ's healing
power to all who desire it.

ii) His divine perception.
In dealing with sickness it is no use just tackling the symptoms; it is vital to get right to the root-cause. This is what
doctors, surgeons, counsellors and all who treat various types
of illness have to strive to do, but it's not always that
straightforward.

When we consider Jesus' ministry it seems that he was
always able to discern the root-cause of any trouble instantly.
He seemed to be able to see behind any mask the real person;
he could see beyond any illness the real cause or barrier to
healing. For example, he was instantly aware that the para-

lysis of the man brought to him by four friends was caused by some sin he had committed,[31] and similarly the blind man he had healed.[32] He knew instantly if the cause of an illness was demon-possession[33,34] and responded with authority. When talking to the rich young man, Jesus knew right away that riches were his 'blockage',[35] and he was able to lightly challenge the woman at the well because he knew everything about her.[36]

Jesus alone had this divine perception which enabled him to reach right to the heart of a person and their trouble or sickness. In our ministry we are bound by our human limitations. Yet we do have the power of God's Holy Spirit to help us to see root-causes, as we shall be discussing in chapter 9.

iii) His methods of healing.

Jesus had no set pattern or method of healing; it seems that he responded variously according to the person, the sickness and the situation. Beyond his constant characteristics of love, care, confidence and authority, we can pick out only one or two other patterns.

He frequently placed his hands on people to heal them, like the blind man at Bethsaida[37] and the crippled woman in the synagogue.[38] Sometimes he touched the afflicted area, as he did for the two blind men[39] and the deaf-mute.[40] It seems that this was a regular feature of his ministry, for it was often what people would expect him to do.[41]

On some occasions he was able to heal by just a word,[42,43] and then at other times over a distance.[44,45] When dealing with the demon-possessed it seems that he would not touch them, but his words were always clear commands.[46,47]

From Jesus' ministry we cannot deduce a single method or pattern of healing for us to follow today. Yet we can pick up a number of his responses to use as guidelines for Christian healing ministry, as later chapters will indicate. However, we can affirm that above all else it must be love, care and faith in God that motivate our ministry, maintained by prayer.

3. Summary

Before moving on to more practical matters, it has been important to ensure that we are absolutely clear about the nature and implications of God's love for us, his total opposition to sickness and suffering of any kind and the pain it must cause him to see any one of his children in illness or agony. I have been concerned to deal with some of the most common misunderstandings about God's attitude to sickness at this stage in order to avoid confusion later on.

In considering particular features of the life and healing ministry of Jesus, not only do we find confirmation of God's overwhelming love and total opposition to sickness, but we are also given a firm foundation upon which to base our thoughts on Christian healing ministry today. As we move on to consider the various aspects of this ministry, we have now a concise picture of the essence of Christ's healing ministry, together with some idea of the ways in which he responded to those who were ill, which will be of considerable value and support in the pages that follow.

One more step is now necessary before we begin our 'journey into a ministry of healing', and that is to consider briefly the ways in which the Apostles took up Christ's healing ministry in the setting of the early Church and then to look at what part that ministry has played in the life of the Church from those early days right up to the present.

Notes

1. Matt. 6:6-15
2. I John 3:1-2
3. Matt. 6:26-30
4. Luke 11:5-13
5. Matt. 6:10, GNB
6. John 1:12-13
7. Matt. 9:1-8
8. John 5:14

9. Mark 8:34
10. Mark 13:9-13
11. e.g. John 9:3
12. e.g. Luke 10:9
13. John 14:7-10
14. Mark 9:29
15. John 9:4
16. John 10:37-38
17. Mark 14:35-36
18. e.g. Luke 10:1-9
19. e.g. Luke 11:9-13
20. e.g. Matt. 9:36 & 14:14
21. e.g. Luke 7:13 & 13:12
22. Mark 7:31-37
23. Mark 8:22-26
24. Mark 1:40-41
25. Mark 2:5
26. Matt. 12:9-14
27. Mark 8:11-12
28. Mark 10:21
29. Luke 13:34
30. John 15:13
31. Mark 2:5
32. John 5:14
33. Matt. 9:32-33
34. Mark 1:21-28
35. Mark 10:17-22
36. John 4:1-30
37. Mark 8:22-26
38. Luke 13:13
39. Matt. 9:29
40. Mark 7:33
41. Mark 7:32 & 8:22
42. Matt. 8:3
43. John 5:8
44. Matt. 8:13
45. Luke 17:13-14
46. Mark 9:25
47. Luke 4:35

Chapter 5

HEALING MINISTRY IN THE CHURCH

'Stretch out your hand to heal, and grant that wonders and miracles may be performed through the name of your holy Servant Jesus' (Acts 4:30 GNB).

1. Healing in the Early Church

Life in the Early Church

The healing ministry, which became such a familiar and significant part of the development of the early Church, has to be seen in the context of the whole of the life of the growing Christian community rather than as a separate concern. It is important therefore to begin by taking a glance at other features of life in the early Church.

As we read through the inspiring chapters of the Acts of the Apostles, a vivid picture emerges of life among the early believers. This way of life is concisely summarised in Acts 2:42-47. Their commitment to one another involved not only sharing in mission and ministry, but also sharing meals together and sharing their material possessions. They would also meet together regularly for times of prayer, praise and learning; there was a great sense of awe amongst their fellowship, and miracles and wonders were commonplace; and the Church was growing fast!

It was through life of deep commitment to God and to one

another that the ministry of healing was able to continue confidently in the early Church.

The Apostles bring Healing

Jesus had not only taught his disciples to oppose sickness just as he did, but he had also spent much of his time in training them to go out and continue the ministry that he had begun. 'Whoever believes in me will do what I do – yes, he will do even greater things, because I am going to the Father,' Jesus had said to them.[1] Then he had clearly commissioned his disciples 'to preach the Kingdom of God and to heal the sick', and had given them the power and authority to do so.[2]

As we read of the dynamic development of the early Church, it is plain to see that they took this command very seriously, opposing sickness with prayerful confidence and authority. Whilst the ministry began with the Apostles,[3] soon it also involved the deacons and other leaders[4] and eventually became very much a shared ministry involving the elders and prayer groups of local churches.[5]

Throughout the Acts of the Apostles we find that preaching and healing are continually linked together as the spearhead of the ministry of the Church.[6] We read that the believers prayed for boldness to carry out their tasks of preaching and healing, and that their prayers were answered![7] It seems that the healing ministry became one of the most vivid ways of preaching their message; not only did the healings attract great attention, but they also provided the springboard for the Apostles to preach the good news of Christ to the eager crowds.

The Apostles were greatly concerned to direct people beyond themselves to Christ.[8] They were well aware that the people could easily make gods out of them[9] and emphasised their own accountability to God and dependence upon Christ.[10] In fact, the whole of their ministry – teaching, preaching, prayer and healing – was entirely 'Jesus-centred'. It was in the name of Jesus that Peter healed the lame man at the Beautiful Gate[11] and the paralysed

Aeneas,[12] and it was to the power of God in Jesus that they continually drew their listeners' attentions.

Beyond this, once again we can find no set pattern or method to the ways in which the healing ministry was continued in the early Church. Peter seems to have been in the habit of using words of command as Jesus often did, and Paul too seemed to have this voice of Christ's authority.[13] Paul was known to have healed by laying his hands on the sick person, in the manner that Jesus had often done, as in the case of the father of Publius.[14] Again, prayer was much at the heart of the Apostles' ministry, as we can see from the account of Peter's healing of Tabitha[15] where he knelt in prayer before directing the dead woman to get up. Healing at a distance also occurred as it had in the ministry of Christ, for we read of people being laid in the streets in order that Peter's shadow might fall on them,[16] and of the handkerchiefs and aprons that Paul had used being taken to the sick – and healing them.[17]

As we have seen, it was not just the original Apostles who healed the sick, for Paul, Barnabas, Stephen and Philip are specifically named as being involved in this ministry. And then by the time that the Letter of James was written, it is clear that prayer for healing was a responsibility of the local church elders too. Thus Christ's healing power was given into the hands of the leaders of the early Church, and they were able to develop this ministry by prayer and confidence in his power to heal.

The Church's Healing Ministry

So far I have focussed on the ministry of the Apostles and other prominent leaders in the early Church. However, it is clear that there were others who had 'gifts of healing'.[18] Healing was recognised as being one of the 'gifts of the Spirit' which was to be used for the building up of the body of the Church. It is probable that Ananias, by whom Paul's blindness was healed, had a gift of healing. Without such a gift he could hardly have had the faith to go to Paul's aid. Thus healing also came through those who had been given a specific gift of healing to use within the ministry of the Church.

From an important little passage in the Letter of James we gather that prayer for healing was very much a part of the ministry of local churches. This passage is well worth quoting, for it has become a basic guideline and justification for the ministry of prayer for healing in the local church today:

> Is any one of you in trouble? He should pray. Is anyone happy? Let him sing songs of praise. Is any one of you sick? He should call the elders of the church to pray over him and anoint him with oil in the name of the Lord. And the prayer offered in faith will make the sick person well; the Lord will raise him up. If he has sinned, he will be forgiven (Jas. 5:13-15 NIV).

It is from these verses that we are given the clearest details of the development of healing ministry in the local setting of the early Church. Here we are given a simple picture of local church leaders visiting sick members to pray for them and anoint them with oil. Through their prayers in faith even sins are forgiven as the sick are restored to health.

Thus the healing ministry had become a normal part of the life of the local church, along with preaching and teaching and all the other aspects which have been mentioned.

2. Healing in the Years that Followed

Days of Decline

We can gather from many of the early Christian writers that the Church's ministry of preaching and healing certainly continued for at least another two hundred years. Although the healing ministry was prominent in the early years, by the end of the third century it occupied very much a back seat compared to the teaching and preaching of the Church.

After the days of persecution, which removed many of the finest and most faithful teachers and leaders, the Church became much preoccupied with setting out clearly its theology and reorganising its structures. The fire and zeal of the past had been overtaken by meticulous teaching and planning, partly as a reaction against the various heresies and deviations which were much in evidence at the time. The true sense of dependence upon God and faith in his power to heal largely faded. Even the practice of praying for healing and anointing with oil seemed to have lost its real purpose, having come to be seen by most merely as a symbolic anointing for the forgiveness of the sins of a sick person who was expected to die. The faith and expectation of God's healing power at work in the Church – so prominent in the life of the early believers – eventually almost vanished away into the past, to become just a part of a wonderful history.

Times of Revival

Over the centuries that followed, whilst the Church continued to show great concern for the sick and dying, to minister to them and pray for their needs, its sense of expectation of any healing was very limited. All too often those who were ill were encouraged to 'bear their cross bravely' in the misguided manner already mentioned. Yet the healing ministry never faded completely.

It was during many of the great times of revival in the Church, when Christian leaders emerged who would turn back to New Testament basics in order to try to renew the Church's ministry, that preaching and healing together once more became the spearhead of Christian ministry. But such movements were always being rejected by the leaders of the Church for one reason or another, and often resulted in division. Apart from such movements – inspired by people like St Francis of Assisi, Martin Luther and John Wesley – the Church's ministry of prayer for healing lay largely dormant until the twentieth century.

3. Christian Healing Ministry in the Twentieth Century

New Movements

It was at the beginning of this century, as the Church began to move forward once more, that the ministry of prayer for healing began to be taken seriously again by a number of Church leaders.

Groups and organisations began to spring up whose concern was the promotion and development of the Church's healing ministry through prayer, sacrament and counselling alongside others involved in the caring and medical professions. Some of the best-known of these societies were the Guild of Health, the Divine Healing Mission (formerly the Society of Emmanuel) and the Guild of St Raphael, all of which were in existence by 1915. A number of personalities did much to encourage and revive the ministry of prayer for healing, including James Moore Hickson of the Divine Healing Mission, who travelled all over the world to encourage this ministry; Dorothy Kerin, who was herself miraculously healed at the point of death and who proclaimed to all that God had healed her and called her to a ministry of healing, eventually leading to the setting up of the Burrswood community of Christ the Healer! and the late George Bennett, renowned for his pioneer work in influencing and encouraging Churches in this ministry all over Britain, Europe and the United States, and also for his earlier ministry with the Divine Healing Mission at Crowhurst.

Soon homes, centres and communities for healing became a vital factor in the growth of the Church's healing ministry, generally working in close co-operation with the other healing professions. Christian healing ministry was becoming firmly established in the wings of the Church, and once again the world was able to see at work the healing hands of God through his people. This time the movement seemed to be spreading through most of the main Christian Churches and was supported rather than condemned by many of the Church's leaders.

In 1944 the Church's Council for Health and Healing held its first meeting on the initiative of Archbishop William Temple. It set out to draw together the many strands of the Church's healing ministry and to encourage both co-operation with the medical profession, and acceptance of this ministry in the Churches.

Since that time, Christian healing ministry has developed and spread into all denominations and to all parts of the world. Most recently it has been fired by the charismatic renewal movement, establishing healing ministry in more and more local churches.

Healing in the Church Today

There can be no doubt that healing is very much a part of the ministry to which Christ is calling his Church today, for it is he who is once more at work in the healing of the sick, through our life and love, through our care and prayer. We are privileged to be living in what I believe to be the Church's most exciting era since New Testament times.

I believe that the ministry of prayer for healing needs to become a natural part of the Church's life and ministry everywhere. We are called to continue this ministry prayer-fully, dedicatedly and quietly, without fuss or display. It is a ministry that we must emphasise, but not over-emphasise lest it become the sole direction of our service. The healing ministry needs to be set alongside the clear teaching and preaching of the Father's unending love for us all, as revealed in the life, death and resurrection of his Son, and as shown by the power of his Holy Spirit, bringing new life into the Church.

Like the leaders of the early Church, we must never forget that it is Christ who does all the healing in the Church – through us. It is to God that all the glory must be given, it is to Jesus Christ that all must be directed and it is by the power of his Holy Spirit that healing comes.

Notes

1. John 14:12
2. Luke 9:1-2
3. Acts 2:43 & 3:1-10
4. Acts 6:8 & 8:6-7
5. James 5:14-15
6. e.g. Acts 3:1-26 & 8:5-8
7. Acts 4:29-31
8. e.g. Acts 3:12-16 & 9:34
9. e.g. Acts 14:8-18
10. Acts 3:11-26
11. Acts 3:6
12. Acts 9:34
13. Acts 14:10 & 16:18
14. Acts 28:7-8
15. Acts 9:36-42
16. Acts 5:12-16
17. Acts 19:11-12
18. I Cor. 12:9 & 28

Chapter 6

JOURNEY INTO A MINISTRY OF HEALING

'The power of the Lord was present for Jesus to heal the sick' (Luke 5:17 GNB).

I hope that these early chapters have encouraged you to see that Christian healing ministry really needs to be at the heart of the life and ministry of every Christian Church. This chapter is concerned with how a church can set about making this possible.

The above quotation from St Luke's Gospel, before the healing of the paralysed man, indicates that there was an awareness among the people in the house that God's power was present in a real and special way for Jesus to heal the sick. Sometimes I have visited churches where I have sensed this feeling of the special presence of God. At St Mark's too, many have sensed God's presence in a special way; either in the church building or through a particular service of prayer for healing. What is this special power and presence of God, and how does it come about that once again Jesus can heal the sick?

1. Preparation

Prayer and Care

It is through faithful prayer, coupled with loving care, that this special power and presence of God in a church or service or group comes about. I see prayer and care as the two pillars upon which any Christian healing ministry must be built. Without prayer and care we will not be open to God to be used by him to bring healing.

As we have seen, Jesus' ministry was rooted in prayer. Prayer was the vital two-way link of communication between Father and Son, which enabled Jesus both to discern God's will and to carry it out.

If prayer was so necessary for Christ's ministry, it follows that our ministry must also be grounded and rooted in prayer. Not only is prayer the only starting-point towards any such ministry of healing, but also it is essential to the maintenance of that ministry. There is no other way in which we can begin or continue.

Yet prayer is even more than this. It is also the channel through which God's power can flow. It is by prayer that God's power is released. Without prayer we remain on our own, and with just our own strength we will bring real healing to no one! To journey into a ministry of healing we must ensure that we make ourselves entirely dependent upon the Father and totally committed to his will. It is his will to bring healing, and it is only by prayer that we can gain and maintain the dependence and understanding that is necessary for his healing power to come to others through us.

We must now go on to look at practical ways of setting up this first pillar, that of prayer. Such prayer needs to be a shared ministry (as I shall explain in chapter 11), therefore it is best to begin by gathering together a group of people who are prepared to commit themselves to meeting regularly, first and foremost to pray together. Sometimes Christian healing ministry has just quietly grown from groups of people who have gathered together faithfully to pray for the sick. In our situation we were forced to pray in a group as the only way that we could cope with the demands being made upon us, but it was from this beginning that prayer for healing grew and developed. I have heard of other groups meeting over long periods to pray patiently for healing ministry to begin. In whatever way the prayer group starts, it remains the best way of building towards a healing ministry.

Soon the members of such a group begin to grow together in openness and commitment to one another, and before long they are likely to be sharing with one another their personal need for prayer. This is good and to be encouraged for it can be the beginning of healing ministry itself, as a deep sense of love and caring for one another develops within the group.

This brings us to the second pillar, and that is care. Unless we really begin to care deeply about one another and about those to whom we are ministering, our prayers are going to be rather hollow. For Christian healing ministry to develop there needs to be a real sense of togetherness with one another and with those we pray for. I can remember when our little prayer group first began to pray with deep commitment for relatives, friends and workmates: over a time it often seemed as if some of those for whom we were praying were also members of the group. How thrilling it was then when we heard of prayers being answered. I remember in particular our prayers for a young wife who longed to have a baby and who had previously suffered much heartache following a number of miscarriages. What wonderful news it was when her baby was born, though only one member of the group actually knew her personally!

A loving, praying fellowship is the best means of establishing prayer for healing. However, it is important to ensure that such a group does not become narrow and introverted or get itself into a rut. The group will need firm leadership, a wide vision and a varied pattern or programme. I offer a possible programme for such a group in the hope that it will only be used as a basis, allowing many variations in content and emphasis.

i) It is always good to begin by looking to the Father in praise and thankfulness. This can be expressed in prayer, in carefully chosen psalms or in the singing of hymns or songs of praise. It is important to try to really feel and express a sense of wonder and thankfulness at God's unending goodness and love.

ii) An appropriate reading from Scripture can offer both inspiration and guidance to the group, possibly with the addition of a *short* thought for the evening.

iii) This could helpfully be followed by silent meditation. It takes time and careful direction for a group to get used to the creative use of silence for listening to God in prayer. At the end of a busy day, it can be difficult to 'tune in', especially as a new experience. Short periods of silence are best at the first few meetings, until the group is able to benefit from longer times of listening-prayer.

iv) The group is then able to move into a time of intercessory prayer together. Guided open prayer is best. To avoid individual prayers that 'go on forever' it can be helpful to suggest that everyone prays using single sentences only. This also encourages those who are not used to this kind of prayer. It is good to begin by looking outward before focussing finally on personal and group needs, and sometimes it can be particularly powerful to join hands in a prayer circle. It can be difficult knowing how to close such times of prayer. Possibly a familiar collect or a quiet, sensitive song offer the best ways.

v) Many groups allow a 'sharing time' before praying. This can be most helpful so long as it doesn't destroy the prayerful atmosphere or become a general discussion instead of prayer!

vi) It is always good to end with space for a chat and a cuppa, for there may be many things that members want to chat with others about.

So we must begin with prayer and care, for it is from these pillars that faith and expectancy, togetherness and love, can soon develop. But our faith and expectancy will not be in anything that *we* might be able to achieve, but in what God can achieve as his love is poured into our hearts, turning prayer into loving care.

Teaching and Learning

If prayer and care were the first two concerns for the

Christians of the early Church, then these were closely followed by teaching and learning. The new members of the fellowship were as keen to learn about Christ as the Apostles were to teach them. It is so easy for church leaders to miss or waste the many teaching opportunities that come our way.

If we are to prepare to embark upon a ministry of prayer for healing, then there are two further important steps to be taken. First of all we must spend time in learning more about the nature of Christian healing ministry, and secondly we need to share this with the whole congregation, using whatever teaching opportunities that arise, in order to begin to build up faith and a greater sense of expectation.

There is now a wide range of helpful books available about Christian healing ministry. (The ones that I have found most helpful are listed in appendix 2 but there are many more.) When working in groups it can be useful to take a particular book to study together, but it is important to make sure that the book is neither too academic nor too narrow for the group. (If you wish to use this book for group study, possible questions for discussion are listed in appendix 1.) On a wider scale the subject might be studied through house groups, Lenten study groups, or a midweek fellowship meeting.

As we learn more, we need to share this with the whole congregation in preparation for the beginning of this ministry. The inevitable reservations about healing ministry are most likely to come from those who would not attend prayer or study groups, therefore it is important that teaching is given in the setting of Sunday services. The Anglican Church Calendar offers a number of opportunities for this (e.g. the eighth Sunday before Easter now has as its theme 'Christ the Healer', and Year II has about six Sunday Gospels based on healing stories. There is also the opportunity of Maundy Thursday, with the Blessing of Oils in cathedrals, which can be used to great advantage). A series of addresses is another possibility, especially if set alongside study in house groups. It is vital that clear teaching about the nature of Christian healing ministry is given in advance to the whole congregation, in order to avoid unnecessary setbacks or even opposition.

I think it is also important to consider carefully the terms that we use. To speak of faith healing, spiritual healing or even of miraculous healing can easily lead to misunderstandings. I have persistently used the terms 'Christian healing ministry' and 'prayer for healing'. To speak of Christian healing ministry is to firmly emphasise that the healing comes from Christ, and use of the term 'prayer for healing' is probably the most sensitive and acceptable introduction.

Finally, it can be a good idea to invite along a guest speaker with more experience of Christian healing ministry, or to take a group of parishioners to a service of prayer for healing in another church. However, care needs to be taken in either case to make sure that you are on the same wavelength. Some years ago I took a small group of church members to a healing service in another church. This turned out to be much more intense and emotional than our own quiet style of ministry and it set back our progress quite a bit. On the other hand, we were able to benefit greatly from a visit from Revd Roy Lawrence and some of his parishioners early on in our ministry. He led us on by focussing our thoughts upon healing prayer and introduced us to new forms of healing meditation, besides offering much helpful advice about the conduct of our healing ministry.

Teaching and learning are essential in preparing for Christian healing ministry, and more than that it is vital that they continue as that ministry develops. We can never know everything about this ministry but we must ensure that we grow to understand all that we can.

Awaiting God's Moment

There is always the temptation to get things moving as quickly as possible and to give insufficient time and care to prayerful preparation. But if we rush on ahead of God our efforts will be of no avail, and things can easily be set back considerably. We must let God lead and await his moment.

I spoke in chapter 3 of the amount of apparent failure that

we encountered in the early stages of our healing ministry through trying to rush on ahead before we were ready, and before God was ready to use us. If we have carefully prepared ourselves and have become sensitive to the Father's leading, then we will be able to cope with any feelings of failure in the early days. It was my decision as pastoral leader to ask God for the sign, that someone should ask for prayers for healing, before we moved on, and in due course that sign was given. Whilst I would not suggest that asking for a sign from God is always the best or only way to begin, I do think that when people are beginning to ask for this ministry – without any pressure from others – it is time to respond to such requests.

I find it helpful to remember that Jesus spent thirty years preparing for just three years of ministry – and what a ministry that was! We should not therefore be concerned if we have to spend a year or so in prayerful preparation before stepping out in such a testing venture of faith and trust in God.

2. First steps

Gentle Beginnings

Having prepared prayerfully and carefully, we now come to the delicate decision about how best the healing ministry can be gently integrated into the wider ministry and worship of the Church. Much prayer and thought needs to be given to this decision, which will be very much dependent upon the local situation. It is important that this ministry is neither tucked away in a quiet corner nor thrust upon an unprepared congregation.

We must think through the question of who is going to take part in the ministry of prayer with laying on of hands and of the nature, time and place of the services. Again much depends on the local situation. The matter of who is to be involved is considered more fully in chapter 11. I would simply mention here that if there are lay members who have been chosen and prepared to share in this ministry with the minister(s), so much the better. They should be formally commissioned, and should be seen to be fully involved from the beginning.

Where and when the first service should be is our next consideration. At St Mark's the route that we had been travelling made it quite natural and right that the first such service should be held in the setting of our midweek fellowship meeting. Soon it became clear that we should move on to midweek services of prayer for healing in the church itself. Finally prayer for healing with laying on of hands became a normal part of our Sunday evening Communion services, with the occasional special service of prayer for healing on Sunday, too. This route of introduction was appropriate to our situation in that the ministry gently broadened out from the fellowship group to the whole congregation. For churches in a similar situation – with a smallish group really ready to begin, but the rest of the congregation not yet prepared – this might be a helpful course to follow. I think, however, that it would normally be better to have many more people in from the start, perhaps by having a course of Sunday evening teaching to the whole congregation which could then be naturally followed up with a Sunday evening service of prayer for healing.

If preparation has been thorough, involving teaching and discussion amongst the whole congregation, then it would be best to begin with a carefully planned evening service in church, possibly on a Sunday and with an experienced guest speaker to help out. However, if there remains any collective feeling that this kind of ministry would be an intrusion into Sunday worship, it might be better to go for a midweek service first of all. Special Sunday services or parts of Sunday services could then be considered when the time seems right.

Roy Lawrence writes: 'There is more to the ministry of Christian healing than an occasional service and a periodic laying on of hands. Christian healing is a way of life, a way of love, a way of prayer, a way of expectant recognition that Jesus is the same yesterday, today and forever.'[1]

For Christian healing ministry to become thus, it cannot be imposed or thrust upon an unprepared and unwilling congregation. We must try to follow with sensitivity whatever course of introduction is most likely to recommend to the whole congregation the ministry of prayer for healing with laying on of hands. By far the most effective way of winning over any doubters or objectors is for them to see their sick friends healed. However, we must then realise that this new ministry is going to radically affect and develop every other aspect of our ministry, too!

Stepping Onwards, in Faith

The journey we have begun will always be a difficult one. Once we have thrown ourselves into God's war against sickness and fought for him in our first battles, we will begin to realise that there are no easy wars or battles. Committed prayer for healing is always costly, with countless unanswered questions, deep anxieties and painful hurts. But then there are also those many moments of sheer joy and wonder at the victory of the Father's healing love.

It will soon appear that some are being healed – usually gradually or after a little time – and others are not. Overconcern at those who are not being healed can soon become the greatest stumbling-block to our stepping onwards in faith. (Reasons why some are not healed will be considered in chapter 10.) In the earliest days of our ministry at St Mark's there seemed to be many more people who were not being healed than who were, and this caused some to feel that we should turn back. I found that when I focussed upon those who were not being healed, I would often feel dejection and doubt, even though they themselves did not seem to have been hurt in any way. But when I focussed on the healings that *were* taking place, I would feel encouraged and determined to go on.

There is always the danger that unwittingly we begin to rely on our own efforts, feeling a sense of inadequacy or failure when some are not healed. However, as time goes by we will not only learn by experience much more about God's ways of healing, but also come to rely more and more on his power. It is therefore crucial that above all else we focus upon the Father's nature, power and promises, as we step onwards in growing faith.

Ways of Praying for Healing

God can use many different ways to bring healing: prayer alone, prayer with fasting, prayer with laying on of hands, prayer with anointing, prayer and counselling, prayer with medication or surgery, and so the list goes on. There is no one successful method or formula by which God's healing comes. Just as Jesus healed in many different ways in New Testament times, so too there are many different ways by which he can heal today. We are able to learn through experience that certain approaches seem best suited to particular situations.

So far I have focussed mainly on the corporate approach to prayer for healing. It is also important that each individual member of any group has a right approach to prayer for healing, for many individual ministers – ordained and lay – will find themselves called upon to pray with and counsel the sick on their own.

Again we must remember, in prayer and in counselling, that it is always the Father's will for his children to be whole and healthy. As we pray for healing, we are not trying to bend God's will or to beg mercy from a cruel father, but rather we must be lining up our will with his will to heal with love. It is thus that we make prayer the channel by which we become really open to God, and through which his healing power can come. We are working with him in the process of healing.

When we pray, therefore, we must pray with confidence in his will to heal. I have often heard the words: 'if it be your will' added on at the end of prayers for the sick. Whilst there are undoubtedly other situations where these words can be appropriate, in healing prayer they are not! It *is* God's will to heal the sick, as we have clearly seen, and the addition of such words just weakens a prayer and can encourage in the sick person feelings of being unloved or rejected by God.

We must also be positive in our prayers. It is far better to focus upon God's power and longing to heal than upon the plight of the sick person. Whilst we should be specific in what we are praying for, we must not in our minds dwell on the problem, but concern ourselves more with the sick person's being well again. Whenever we dwell upon trouble, it always seems to grow worse; if, instead, we dwell upon God's healing power, then, as that becomes strong, sickness diminishes.

Finally, we must pray with loving commitment. Vague or general prayers will neither be effective nor encourage the sick person to feel accepted, loved and cared for either by God or by us. If we pray with real commitment and confidence, then God's love and care will be seen clearly and effected powerfully.

3. Problems and Misunderstandings

Problems and Objections

Throughout his ministry Jesus found himself dogged by those who objected to everything he was doing. These were many of the religious leaders of his day who felt threatened by the powerful effects of his ministry, and who were determined to do all they could to condemn his words and works and discredit him. Their objections were many: he was drawing people away from the true Jewish Law, beliefs and practices; he had no official authority to heal; he was working on the Sabbath – by healing; he had no right to forgive sins; and there was even the suggestion that he was a disciple of the 'Prince of Devils' from whom he gained his power. In vain they strove to discredit him in the eyes of the public: people were far more aware of the power of his teaching and healing than of the petty objections of the religious leaders.

Fortunately we are hardly likely to encounter such hostility as this. However, we do need to be aware of the likelihood that some of our own congregation may object to healing ministry, and that they will probably be some of those who have rather traditional views about ministry and worship. Whilst objections and objectors can be very frustrating, they can be used creatively if we respond caringly to those who object and carefully and clearly to their objections.

I would like to look briefly at some of the most common objections, and how we might respond to them. I think the most common fear is of emotionalism, or even hysteria, and that healing ministry is just another trendy kind of public display to fill up our churches once again! In our society we are generally discouraged from revealing our true emotional feelings in public, whether these are joys or heartaches, and this in itself can be a cause of stress illnesses. This has also led to inhibited ways of worshipping God in church. Only limited expression of our love for God, our joy and excitement, is regarded as acceptable. Whilst this is sad, it has led others to overreact to the situation with ways of worship that can be too emotional, showy or unreal. Christian healing ministry is never just an 'emotional trip' – it is a healing touch from Christ himself. However, such an encounter is bound to affect our emotions, for time and again I find those who have been healed are thrilled at their healing and longing to tell others. This is entirely natural and rather like the experience of the child who has just come top in an exam, or the married couple who have just had their first child.

Nearly all the services of prayer for healing that I have ever been to have been gentle, quiet and reverent occasions, without any showiness or display, often with something of the feel of a rather special Communion service. This gentle and quiet approach was Jesus' way, and it needs to be ours too. In this, as in all forms of worship, we need to feel natural and relaxed, and services of prayer for healing need to reflect much of the normal pattern of life and worship in the local church.

As to the matter of this ministry being geared towards filling up churches, it is important to point out that love and care for people, and longing to bring healing because it is God's will that we should, must be our motives from the beginning. Many are bound to come to faith through being healed, and this makes for true wholeness, but we must not set out to use this ministry as a means of filling up pews. If we do, we will fail!

I have often heard concern expressed that people are likely to get hurt or to lose faith if they are not healed. Some would feel that this danger – of people being built up to expect healing and then let down if they don't receive it – is sufficient to prevent further steps in healing ministry. I must admit that this was also one of my reservations at first. However, I believe that this reluctance was the product of my own self-dependence rather than dependence upon God's loving power. I know of no one who has been deeply hurt or has lost faith through not being healed. Furthermore, almost everyone who *is* healed seems to grow tremendously in personal faith and commitment to God.

Doubts and Misunderstandings

Besides various objections there are also bound to be doubts and misunderstandings that occur, however much trouble we may have taken to offer clear teaching, and these too must be sensitively dealt with.

'It's all in the mind,' I sometimes hear people say when trying to explain someone else's illness or healing. It is very true that a tremendous number of physical illnesses stem from stresses and anxieties in the mind, as we will shortly see, but a healing of the mind is no less a healing than a healing of the body. What is most important is the fact that the healing comes not from our own efforts or attitudes but from the healing touch of Christ, supported by our own mental co-operation.

Sometimes people feel that healing ministry should only be conducted by specially gifted priests or laymen, and many ministers encourage this view by sending sick parishioners to others who exercise this ministry. This was not the practice encouraged in the Letter of James; the elders of the Church were certainly not all either gifted or ordained. At St Mark's we know of no one in the congregation who has a special gift of healing, and I am the only ordained minister. Yet the ministers and elders lay hands on many people who are then healed, and it seems to make no difference at all who is involved in the laying on of hands.

Sometimes I can sense a fear in people's minds, either about the nearness of God or about his supernatural power. They react as if healing ministry is something we shouldn't meddle in, as if it's dangerous and going against God's will, rather like a mischievous child meddling with an electric power-point. Others have suggested that there's something sinister or even evil about it all. Jesus faced this problem too, when it was claimed that he received his power from the 'Prince of Devil's'.[2] The former objection stems from a wrong image of God, as a stern, distant and prohibitive parent in the Victorian mould, rather than as a loving father who longs to heal his children, as Jesus proved! The second objection is usually rooted in doubts about other non-medical forms of healing. We must remember that not all healing necessarily comes from God. There are many apparent healings through 'gifted people' and groups that are not Christian. The question I always need to ask about a 'faith healer' or 'spiritual healer' is, 'where does the power to heal come from?' Unless we are sure that it comes from God, through Christ, then such healing should be strictly avoided, for it is this that can counterfeit and discredit true Christian healing ministry.

A final misunderstanding is that we are setting up this ministry in opposition to the medical service. Nothing could be further from the truth. God has many ways of healing, not only by prayer but also by medicine and surgery. We must do all that we can to work in close co-operation with those involved in the medical profession, as I shall be explaining in chapter 8. Many of the wonderful healings that we have seen (including my own) have come about through medical means, backed up by committed prayer.

Notes

1. Roy Lawrence – *Invitation to Healing* (p. 103.)
2. Mark 3:20-30

Chapter 7

THE PLACE OF FAITH

'The apostles said to the Lord, "Make our faith greater."
The Lord answered, "If you had faith as big as a mustard
seed, you could say to this mulberry tree, 'Pull yourself up
by the roots and plant yourself in the sea!' and it would
obey you"' (Luke 17:5-6 GNB).

1. What is Faith?

When Jennifer came to her first healing service, it was not
with a great sense of hope and expectation. She was not a
person of any great faith but, in her own words, she was
'grasping for something'. And yet a member of the congregation approached her as she arrived at the church to tell her
that she believed God was going to heal her.

It seemed this might be stretching faith a little too far, for it
was now well over forty years since the motor-cycle accident
which had shattered Jennifer's life. A fractured femur, pelvic
injuries, crushed toes and other injuries to legs and feet had
left Jennifer permanently disabled and lame. The worst and
most painful injuries were those to one of her feet: she had
been left unable to move it in any way and it was like a solid
block, causing daily pain. Specially-made surgical shoes had
enabled her to get about a little, but she could walk neither
far nor fast because of the pain. Shoes were always a problem
for her as she had to walk on the side of her foot, and this used
to lead to further problems of stiffness in her ankle. Pain-
killers seemed to be the only source of relief and she took

them daily. She had often passed by the church, and had longed to come to a service, but she was just too shy. Then, one day, she had met one of our pastoral visitors who had invited her along, and for some months now she had been coming each Sunday.

Today Jennifer had come along for the first time to a service of prayer for healing. Would God be able to do anything for her? She enjoyed the service and was encouraged at just the possibility of some measure of healing. At the bidding she went forward for prayer for healing, and soon experienced a feeling of warmth all over. But her journey home was just as painful as the journey to the church had been.

For the next three weeks there was little improvement, but Jennifer continued to come to Sunday services. It was twenty-five days after the healing service, having just returned home from the Sunday evening Communion service, that Jennifer saw the first signs of her healing. She had taken off her shoes and was sitting in front of the fire warming her feet, when she noticed that her bad foot seemed more straight than usual. Then, as she sat there, her toes actually began to move for the first time since the accident. She couldn't believe it! As she looked closer she could even see bones moving, and within moments movement began to come back into her whole foot. She stood up and tried her foot on the floor – again for the first time – and found that she could walk with the flat of her foot on the ground. She was thrilled and excited and longed to rush out and tell someone, but there was no one around to tell until the next day. It seems that the healing received at the healing service had actually been put into motion through the Communion service that day. Although she had initially received healing it had not become evident to her until then.

Jennifer's relief from pain was instant. Pain-killers were set aside and each day her foot got a little better and stronger. Her faith began to grow in leaps and bounds, and so did her healing – but she had her challenges too: friends in the local community who had known her for years tended to be sceptical and some just refused to believe her. Even though she knew that she was so much better, these doubts came as a difficult challenge, and some would really hurt her. Even one or two church members seemed a little doubtful. But Jennifer knew that she would never forget the moment when, sitting in front of the fire, she had seen her foot moving for the first time. In due course she went for her regular check-up with her doctor. He was amazed! Although unable to account for the sudden change, he confirmed that there had been incredible improvement.

Today Jennifer is a new woman. No longer does she hobble about everywhere; now she has just a slight limp. She uses her new mobility well, in taking on all kinds of useful tasks to help others, and also in doing a little home-visiting from time to time. And she can even join in a little dancing now and again!

Faith clearly played a part in her healing. There was the faith of those who prayed for her healing, the faith of the lady who believed Jennifer would be healed and then the faith of Jennifer herself as she overcame the many doubts of those around her in believing God was healing her. All of this faith has been greatly rewarded!

Within Christian healing ministry there is no doubt that faith has an important part to play. Whilst faith itself cannot effect healing, and we cannot 'earn' healing by our faith, there is no doubt that faith in Christ does seem to make us more open to receive his healing. The presence of faith is a powerful agent in enabling the full flow of Christ's healing power, whether that faith be in the heart of the sick person, of the 'ministers', or even of a third person.

Jesus' Faith

In considering the place of faith in Christian healing minis-try, we begin by looking at the place of faith in Jesus' ministry. His faith in his Father was clearly his mainstay. This absolute faith enabled him not only to trust in God for all things, but also to maintain an unbreakable bond with the Father. When it came to responding to the sick, he knew that it was the Father's will that he should heal, and he knew that he had been given the power to effect that will – every time. In Jesus' entire dependence upon the Father, and in his confidence in God's will and power to heal, we see complete faith. We see a quality of trust and love that stems from oneness with the Father and full knowledge of his will.

We cannot have the knowledge of God that Jesus had, and we will never be able to match his faith. But the wonderful thing is – we don't need to! He has faith for us. He asks of us only 'faith as big as a mustard seed',[1] and he told all of his followers simply to trust in God, through him.[2] This was his teaching both to his disciples and to those who came to him for healing: that their little bit of faith in him could open the way for his total faith in God to heal!

Whilst there were times when it seemed that Jesus' faith alone enabled healing,[3,4] there is no doubt that he was keen to look for faith in others. Often he would ask those who came for healing whether they had faith in his power to heal;[5,6] at other times he would just look for signs of faith.[7,8] He seemed keen to commend and encourage the faith of those who were healed,[9,10] or of third parties who came in faith to ask for the healing of another.[11,12] Jesus taught his followers much about the importance and effectiveness of faith; that they should pray in faith,[13] and that whatever they asked in his name they would receive.[14]

Jesus' faith in the Father and oneness with him was the foundation of his ministry. In faith he was able to heal all who came to him. Although he often commended the faith of those who came to him, it was not their faith that actually healed. Jesus himself did the healing, whilst their faith may have been the factor that opened up the way for his healing power to flow. Today it is still Christ who heals through his Church. Our faith can only open up the way for him to heal.

A Church's Faith

Jesus had so demonstrated his own faith, and built up the faith of his disciples, that we see this same pattern of faith continued in the life and ministry of the early Church. The

Apostles always had faith when they healed, faith in the power of Jesus,[15] and sometimes faith was also seen in those who were healed,[16] or again in third parties.[17] In the church's corporate ministry, we read in the Letter of James that the elders' prayer for the healing of a sick person was to be made in faith[18] and that the sick person would be healed.

It follows therefore that within the Church today the presence of faith is our greatest asset in opening up the way for Christ to heal once more. Unless we put our faith and trust in God's loving will to heal through his Son, then we as his Church cannot begin to bring his healing to the sick. As small groups of people come together in the first faltering steps of faith, and focus on God's loving power and will to heal, then faith must begin to grow and spread, through the Church. Faith and confidence in God's will to heal must radically affect our attitudes to all kinds of illness.

Dorothy was on her way to a prayer meeting when the severe chest pains began. By the time she arrived she was in great pain and a nurse who was present realised that she was suffering a heart-attack. Whilst someone went to phone for an ambulance, the rest of the group began to pray for her with laying on of hands. Immediately she began to feel the pain easing and draining away. By the time the ambulance reached the house she was much better, and upon her arrival at the hospital it was confirmed that she had indeed had a slight heart-attack. She was kept in hospital for a few days and then allowed home. She has been well ever since. What power there is when a group of Christians pray in faith for healing!

Personal Faith

John was working in the church climbing up and down ladders. Occasionally he had been troubled by rheumatic pains in his right knee, and once again they began to cause him pain. He quietly knelt down there and then and asked God to heal the trouble. He simply had sufficient faith to ask. Then he got up again and returned to his work, soon forgetting all about the pain and his prayer. It was some time later, after he had left the church to get on with other work elsewhere, that he realised that the pain had gone, and he thanked God. That was some months ago, and he has not been seriously troubled since.

Most Christians tend to be very much aware of the weaknesses in our own personal faith, and we are liable to use these as excuses from time to time. But we can achieve nothing by our faith alone. Our small trust must be focussed firmly on the power and love of God, and not on the strength of our faith! Whilst Jesus so often looked for faith in those who came to him for healing, he did not try to measure that faith, even though for some it was probably no more than a desperate cry for help. Even with such limited faith, Jesus was able to effect healing.

Because a person might have great faith, it does not necessarily follow that he will be healed in the way that he asks. Because another person has little or even no faith, it does not follow that he will not be healed. Whilst faith can sometimes be the vital factor that opens the way for Christ to heal, it does not actually effect the healing. Christ does that! However, I do believe that everyone who comes forward in faith to ask Christ to heal can be sure that he will respond in love. Healing may not be instant, may not be in the manner that we expect, nor even evident for a time, but I do not believe that Jesus could turn anyone away empty-handed when they have approached him in faith. That is not the pattern of his ministry in the Gospels. We cannot know *how* he will respond to those who ask in faith, but we can be sure that he *will* respond – with deep love and care. When we come to him *in faith* we are more open to his healing power; but it is not *by our faith* that we are healed; it is by Jesus!

Faith is trust in God's power and love. If we concern ourselves too much with the quality and strength of our faith in God, then we are not likely to get very far in Christian healing ministry, and may well be forced to give up in despair at an early stage. If, instead, we focus on God's faith in us, on his loving power and firm promises to us, by using the limited faith that we have to pray in obedience for those who are sick, then God will certainly respond and our faith will begin to grow. I have heard it said that it is not so much great faith that we need as faith in God's greatness! If we are certain of God's greatness, his deep love for us and his power to heal, then the way is open for that healing power to flow, however weak our faith may actually seem.

2. Faith versus Fear

The Prayer of Faith

When we look closely at Jesus' teaching about prayer and faith, we find some quite remarkable promises:

> Ask, and you will receive; seek, and you will find; knock, and the door will be opened to you. For everyone who asks will receive (Matt. 7:7-8 GNB).

> When you pray and ask for something, believe that you have received it, and you will be given whatever you ask for (Mark 11:24 GNB).

> If you had faith as big as a mustard seed, you could say to this mulberry tree, 'Pull yourself up by the roots and plant yourself in the sea!' and it would obey you (Luke 17:6 GNB).

> And so the Father will give you whatever you ask of him in my name (John 15:16 GNB).

This teaching is echoed throughout the Gospels, and if we link it all together we can see that Jesus promised that if we prayerfully ask the Father for anything, in his name, and we really believe in faith that we have already received it, then we will have received it. We find this teaching confirmed and used in the life of the early Church. The Letter of James points out: 'When you pray you must believe and not doubt at all.' (1:6) And James also links this theme to the ministry of prayer for healing: 'This prayer made in faith will heal the sick person,' (5:15).

It is quite plain then that the prayer of faith is seen as a prayer which involves believing that we have actually received what we are asking, and thanking God for it, no matter how else things may appear.

It was the prayer of faith that was prayed by Barbara (see pp. 38–39). She began to thank God for healing the overpowering grief of bereavement, even though she actually felt no better, and in due course she was able to experience that healing. If we can picture the Father's deep joy when we pray in faith knowing that he will respond in love, then we begin to understand the effectiveness of the prayer of faith. It is a matter of trusting in God's love and believing in his promises, rather than in what we might see or feel.

However, there are those who have prayed to God for healing, firmly believing that he would do as they asked, and he has not. So what is the problem? I believe there are two further considerations which need to be borne in mind.

First of all we must see Jesus' promises in the wider context of the teaching in which they were given, that of our submission to the sovereign will of God. The need for our asking to be in dependence upon God, through Christ, is emphasised in John's Gospel: 'If you remain in me and my words remain in you, then you will ask for anything you wish, and you shall have it' (John 15:7 GNB).

The prayer of faith needs to be God-centred and not self-centred, or else we will have begun to adopt a 'genie of the lamp' attitude towards God. Any suggestion of our manipulating him, of our telling him what to do and how and when to do it, is turning the context of his promises upside-down. It is *we* who must live so that *his* will may be done, and not he who must bow to ours!

As a father I try to give my children what is best for them. My two youngest are forever asking for sweets but are now growing to realise that they will rarely get them on demand. If I always gave in to their requests then they would soon become spoilt and even more demanding. They would be able to manipulate me, and would soon come to regard me merely as a provider rather than as a loving father. However, it is when we are just enjoying being out together or doing something together that the sweets, ice-creams or even little presents are more likely to be forthcoming. It is when it is set in that sort of loving father/child context that the prayer of faith can be most effective. God's response may not be exactly as we have asked, nor even when we have asked, but he *will* respond. That is the promise!

The second consideration is that we must trust that the Father, in his great love for us, always knows best what is good for us. It is in that knowledge – which we do not have – that he will respond. If my son asks for a birthday party, I may well have to say no, especially if I have some other rather special treat in mind. It is in that knowledge – which he does not have – that I cannot agree to exactly what he is asking for. Sometimes there are reasons of which *we* are not aware that prevent God's doing exactly as we are asking. There are many such blocks to healing which we cannot understand.

However, let us not take anything away from these great promises which inspire the prayer of faith. If we believe that the Father will always respond in love and do what is best for us, then we can pray the prayer of faith with confidence, and we can expect action! This may be complete healing, or perhaps the strength to cope with trouble or suffering, but always that sense of love, joy and peace that is God's certain response to the believer's prayer of faith.

Doubts and Fears

Doubts and fears are the most cunning opponents of the prayer of faith. Just as it is faith that builds up our dependence upon God, our child-like trust in his loving care, so it is doubts and fears which seek to break it all down.

We are all susceptible to the kinds of doubts and fears that cause us to worry, to become depressed, or to try to get by on our own instead of focussing upon God and upon his loving power and promises. While faith looks to God, fear causes us to feel isolated and alone. Fear can sever our prayer-communication with God, while faith increases our prayerful trust!

Lack of faith, or giving in to doubts and fears, is a frequent block to healing. Set over against the prayer of faith we find the fear of really trusting in God. This fear can be fed by our lack of knowledge of the full nature of God – his love, his power and his longing to heal – and this is why I have been at such pains to clarify our view of the nature and will of the Father.

At St Mark's we have sometimes found ourselves faced with doubts and fears. In the early days, we began to feel surrounded by sickness; wherever we looked people seemed to be ill. Fear told us that we couldn't cope and that it would be foolish to go on; faith directed us to trust in God, as he *could* cope, and thus we were able to move on. Much later it began to seem that St Mark's healing ministry had 'dried up'. For a year, just prior to the service outlined in chapter 2, hardly any healings seemed to have taken place. Doubt suggested that God had somehow withdrawn his healing power; faith indicated that we had drawn away from him, that we were no longer fully dependent upon God, and should look to him anew for strength. In fact we came to realise that we had gone astray not only by becoming less dependent upon God, but also by failing to treat this ministry with the sense of special-ness that we should. Instead of constantly thanking God for such a precious and wonderful gift, we had begun to take the healing ministry for granted, trusting more in our own efforts than in God's loving power. Thankfully, after much prayer-ful self-examination and new submission to God, the healing ministry resumed.

Doubts and fears are best conquered by focussing on God; by depending upon his loving power and promises.

Andrea had always had a fear of anything to do with hospitals, and even a visit to the dentist would unnerve her. Soon she was to undergo a major operation and the thought of anaesthetics and the operating theatre was already begin-ning to make her quite ill; she couldn't eat and was suffering frequent tummy upsets. Fear was gaining the upper hand, so she turned to God for help. Quietly she prayed through the 'Ring of Peace' (see chapter 2) on her own. Things seemed easier. She prayed it through many times again, and gradually all her fear and nervousness began to disappear. By the time she came to be admitted, she was able to accept it quite cheerfully, and even at the moment of going down for the operation her fear had not returned. The operation went well, she recovered very quickly, and she is no longer afraid of hospitals!

Fear is the persistent enemy of faith. Faith and fear are forever locked in combat, but only faith comes from God. Most healings seem to be gradual, as faith steadily overcomes fear. Sometimes, however, a person who has been fully healed can allow fear in again at the first setback. It has been my experience that most people who are healed seem to face a little setback or challenge before very long, something that turns out to be a kind of test of their faith. Unless that person turns to God instead of worrying about the challenge, then the healing can be reversed. About three weeks after Don had been healed (see pp. 44–47), he awoke one morning to find that all his worries and troubles had returned, and he felt he was back where he had started. Fortunately his wife took the initiative and they turned to God to pray that the cloud would lift. It took a great deal of prayer, but by the next day Don was fine again. This pattern has repeated itself a number of times since then, but Don has always come through by pushing aside his doubts and fears to turn to God in prayer for help.

Doubts and fears will remain our constant enemy, but faith in God is by far the stronger. Whilst fear can wreak havoc in our ministry, faith brings stability and confidence.

Faith and Common Sense

I have written of how to pray the prayer of faith and set aside doubts and fears. I feel that I must also add a few words about the natural gift of common sense and how we must always use it.

It is in the early days of being involved in Christian healing ministry that our confidence and faith is likely to be weakest, and our understanding of God's ways of working to be most limited. This is when we are liable to make mistakes, by trying to run before we can walk. We need to be careful to move on at God's pace, not to wrest the initiative from him, but to act in accordance with our growing faith and understanding. We need to be aware that there are many blocks to healing within and beyond our knowledge, and it is foolish to assure people that they have been healed exactly as they expect unless we can be absolutely confident about it through some word from God.

As time goes by, those involved in Christian healing ministry begin to be able to sense those who are most likely to be healed and we are able to give greater encouragement. For example, I can be confident in telling those who come to St Mark's with headaches or migraines that they should expect to be healed, for I know of no one with this kind of complaint who has not been healed. On the other hand, I am equally aware that I cannot speak with such confidence to a person in the advanced stages of some form of cancer. I know well that God *can* heal anyone, and that such a person may indeed be healed, but I am also aware that the healing may not be in the manner we ask. We must always move forward trusting in God's power and longing to heal, but we can never predict precisely how he will respond. What we do know is that he *will* respond in his perfect love.

I must also mention that there is such a thing as a 'gift of faith'.[19] This occurs when a person is given knowledge from God that healing is going to take place (as it was given to the lady who approached Jennifer at the beginning of this chapter). This is a special gift which seems to be given from time to time to certain Christians in order that God may reveal his intentions. It is a gift that people tend to grow in, as they become able to recognise with confidence that God is speaking to them. The 'gift of faith' lies in accepting this knowledge without hesitation, and then praying with trust that the person is going to be healed. This gift is not given to many and needs to be used with great care.

Apart from this, we must always use the natural gift of common sense as we seek God's guidance in ministering to the sick. This is not lack of faith, for lack of faith is submission to doubts and fears. Faith and common sense go hand in hand as we move on in trusting dependence upon God's great power to heal.

3. Hope and Expectancy

Growing in Faith

I was never trained to expect miracles. I believed that if I worked hard by caring for people and helping them to grow as Christians, then God would bless my ministry. I think my faith was as much in me and my own abilities as it was in God, although I had long been firmly committed to his service. I didn't think about my faith too often, because when I did it seemed rather weak and inferior. Little did I realise at the time that this recognition is the very point at which faith in God can begin to grow. For faith is realising and accepting our own weakness, and relying instead upon God's strength. It is as we begin to do this that faith in God begins to grow.

Faith needs to be a growing thing. Jesus was always talking about growing things in his parables. Faith the size of the tiniest mustard seed is enough, he said, for if that faith is fed and nurtured it will grow strong and bear much fruit. As we focus more on God's greatness, especially through the New Testament, we can learn to trust more in him than in ourselves, and can begin to see his power at work in the present, in healing and in many other ways.

Faith is a spreading thing. When fear takes hold it can spread like a forest fire, seizing everyone but then soon burning itself out. Faith spreads more slowly through a congregation, as people grow in hope, expectancy and then confidence in God and his power and will to heal. Faith is much more of a lasting thing, too. Those who are very ill can soon find themselves in the grip of fear. The more ill they are, the greater that fear becomes, and the harder to overcome with faith. But if as a Church we continually display firm faith in God's will and power to heal, then faith will grow and spread everywhere as people gain in the confidence that God can and will heal.

Jerry had grown much in faith and was well aware of God's power to heal. When he began to pass blood in his urine he didn't panic. He just trusted in God, prayed about the situation and went to see his doctor. He was sent to the hospital for tests, where they diagnosed a large stone in the kidney and blocked tubes leading from kidney to bladder. An operation seemed likely, but more tests would have to be taken beforehand to assess the extent of the trouble. Jerry came home, offered his situation to God and asked a number of his friends to pray for him too. Soon he was called for the further tests. When the results came through, it was revealed that the blockage in the tubes had cleared and the stone now seemed to be much less of a problem. He was discharged, and we thanked God together for his loving care.

Growing in Dependency

As we grow in faith, so too we grow in dependency upon God. Becoming more aware of our own shortcomings makes us more dependent upon God for everything. It was in such dependency that Jesus began his ministry, praying and fasting in the wilderness. From time to time prayer with fasting can be a really helpful way of acknowledging and expressing our dependency upon God. Much teaching about fasting can be found in the Gospels,[20] and there is a fine book by Arthur Wallis, *God's Chosen Fast*, which deals with the whole matter very thoroughly. Here I just want to mention a few important practical details.

We fast not to change God's will, to twist his arm, but rather to acknowledge our entire dependence upon him. It is an act of commitment to God, rather than something to add force to pleas or demands. Fasting is only for those who are sufficiently healthy to be able to abstain from food (not drink) for a time. I find it helpful to fast for twenty-four hours before a service of prayer for healing, or to fast by missing a couple of meals before going to pray with someone who is seriously ill. It can also be helpful to fast for a day each week for a time, as an act of commitment. For fasts of more than twenty-four hours, I would suggest that a little more knowledge about ways and effects of fasting is necessary. Fasting makes us better channels of God's power and love; we become stronger by our increased dependency on Him. That empty feeling inside is not only a constant reminder of that dependence, but also becomes a constant call to prayer. Fasting always needs to be coupled with prayer to be of real effectiveness in our ministry. After fasting I have found myself to be more alert to God, more in tune with his will, and more dependent upon him for everything.

I believe that it is also important to be dependent upon God's Holy Spirit for guidance in matters of understanding and counselling those who are ill. As I have had little training in these fields I am well aware of my own shortcomings and I find that this increases my dependence upon God. Time and again when talking with those who are sick or depressed I find myself at a loss as to the cause of the problem and how I should respond. I have found that prayer beforehand, during our conversations (in whatever manner is possible) and then afterwards can often enable God to lead us to the heart of a problem, and to begin the healing process. I will mention more about this in chapter 9. As dependency upon God increases, so he is able to work more effectively through each of us to bring healing.

The Faith that God will Respond

I have considered the prayer of faith and its consistent and powerful effect; I have emphasised the importance of turning away from doubts and fears to focus upon God; and I have indicated some of the ways by which we can grow in faith and dependence upon him. As we grow in this faith and dependence, we must always expect with absolute certainty that God will respond to our every prayer and need.

The more we become lined up with the Father's will and open to his leading, the more clearly we will come to know what to ask of him and how to look for his response. Whilst we can never know for certain what will be the manner and timing of his response, we can begin to see how and where to look, because we are completely certain that he *will* respond.

Andrew and his wife were called to the hospital urgently. His sister-in-law, who was in her early fifties, had been taken ill and was on the danger list. She had a mild heart condition, but now her lungs had filled up with fluid. She was on oxygen, no one could go in to see her, and there was little hope. As the family gathered outside the ward to wait, there was a feeling of uneasiness and helplessness. Only Andrew and his wife were Christians, but he suggested that they should all pray quietly for his sister-in-law's recovery. They prayed on and off from midnight until 5 a.m. in the morning: they prayed for her recovery, they prayed for relief from anxiety and then they just left everything in God's loving hands. By the time they were ready to leave she had begun to improve steadily. She was off the critical list and they were allowed in to see her. Everyone felt a tremendous sense of thankfulness and relief. Three weeks later she was home again, fit and well, and she has since been completely discharged. When we pray together in the faith that our loving Father will respond, then we can be sure that our faith will not be in vain!

Notes

1. Luke 17:6
2. John 14:11-14
3. e.g. Luke 7:11-17
4. e.g. John 5:1-9
5. e.g. Matt. 9:28
6. e.g. Mark 9:23
7. e.g. Luke 18:35-43
8. e.g. John 9:6-7
9. e.g. Mark 5:34
10. e.g. Luke 17:19
11. e.g. Matt. 8:10
12. e.g. Mark 5:36
13. Matt. 21:22
14. John 15:16
15. e.g. Acts 3:6 & 9:34
16. e.g. Acts 14:9
17. e.g. Acts 9:38
18. James 5:15
19. see I Cor. 12:9
20. e.g. Matt. 6:5-18

Chapter 8

HEALING AND WHOLENESS

'I have come in order that you might have life – life in all its fullness' (John 10:10, GNB).

1. The Whole Person

Our Whole Make-up

God is concerned with much more than just a person's physical health; he cares about every part of us. Jesus did not just heal illnesses of the body; he was also concerned to deal with problems of an emotional or spiritual nature, some of which were the causes of physical illness anyway.

Jesus' healing ministry was frequently accompanied with preaching and teaching about the life of fullness or wholeness, centred upon a right relationship with God. He spent a tremendous amount of his time with those who were regarded as the outcasts and sinners of his day. When a physical illness had a spiritual cause, he would point this out, as in the cases of the healings or two paralytics.[1,2] Others he encountered had emotional problems, like Peter, or relationship problems, like the woman at the well. (See chapter 9.) Others again were possessed by evil spirits, like the man in the synagogue,[3] and the Gadarene demoniacs,[4] and these too were liable to lead to other problems of spiritual, emotional and physical illness.[5]

We must follow Christ's example and also preach and teach about the life of wholeness, life in all its fullness. In his concern for the whole person, Jesus always had the knowledge to perceive precisely what was the root-cause of any problem or illness, and he knew exactly how to deal with it. Similarly, we must be at pains to search out root-causes, with God's help, so that we are not merely dealing with symptoms. We must also be careful not to make wrong diagnoses, as this can lead to a completely wrong approach which could cause a great deal of harm (e.g. trying to cast out spirits that don't exist from a person with emotional problems!).

So Christian healing ministry is much more than bringing physical healing. It involves emotional stability, spiritual holiness and freedom from evil influences. The ultimate goal is wholeness.

The Stresses of Today

Over the past hundred years or so, tremendous strides have been made in the prevention and cure of many of the previously notorious killer-diseases such as tuberculosis, smallpox, pneumonia, diphtheria and polio. Yet we still find surgeries and hospitals full to overflowing with people suffering from new kinds of illnesses, in particular depression, worry, tiredness, insomnia, headaches and phobias.

Just as the nature of illnesses has changed so dramatically, so too has much of the treatment. Various kinds of tablets and drugs are being taken by more and more patients to ease the symptoms, and doctors involved in seeking the causes of these illnesses are well aware that these new problems stem mainly from our present-day way of life. Some of the most deadly illnesses like cancers are very much affected by what we eat, drink (and smoke), and by the changing highly-polluted environment we live in. Other illnesses, like heart diseases and many of those mentioned above, including cancers, can be the effects of the pressures and stresses of everyday life today. It has been rightly said by many in the medical fields of research that the relation between body and

mind is the cause and cure of disease. 'As man is body, mind
and spirit, and health depends on the harmonious functioning of the whole man, the task of medicine and the Church
are inseparable; co-operation thus comes into line with
Christ's charge to his disciples to heal and preach.' (From
BMA Committee report on 'Divine Healing and Co-
operation between Doctors and Clergy', 1956.)

Whilst on the one hand our modern-day way of life in the
West is made easier and more enjoyable through the avail-
ability of so many domestic and social facilities, on the other
hand never have there been so many pressures and stresses to
cope with – at home, at work and even in social life. Never
has our Western world been so full with so many tired people!
At work there are pressures of ambition, success or maybe
survival; alternatively there may be the threat of redundancy
or the disaster of being unemployed. At home, women face
pressures of other kinds: bringing up children without all the
old family-support systems, oppressive housing, loneliness,
boredom, feelings of being trapped, or even the added responsibilities of having to cope with the frustrations of an
unemployed husband. Many more marriages are falling
apart as partners seek escape in a new start, heaping new
tensions on to the whole family. Children suffer through tired
parents, too-busy parents, impatient parents, frustrated parents or separated parents. For many people there just don't
seem to be sufficient hours in the day; for many others there is
more time on their hands than they can cope with. Even as
we try to relax at home, instead of just enjoying one another's
company we tune in to the pressures that television has to
offer. We find ourselves not only pounded with all the
national and international disasters, threats and problems,
but also pressurised to change and develop our lifestyles.
Good news and honest entertainment have now become rare
commodities.

Even as I write about our twentieth century Western
world, I begin to feel tired and depressed. Why? Because if
we focus on all the problems and pressures of our troubled
times, they are bound to seem worse. Just as those who are ill

deteriorate if they dwell upon their illness, so too our troubles seem to grow worse the longer we gaze at them. We need a new and healing point of focus. Some seek this in tablets, alcohol or various other kinds of drugs, but the relief they offer is only temporary; the problems return seeming worse than ever. Others find new social outlets to give a few hours of relief, and some seek new personal relationships. For most, however, the idea of a life of fullness or wholeness seems no more than a paper dream – yet still they chase after it!

Our Needs – to be Healthy

The stresses of life today expose every human weakness. In some way or other, everyone seems to be in need of healing. We must recognise that the greatest cause of sickness today is stress.

To do this, we must encourage people to turn away from their problems and illnesses (remembering that the more we focus upon them, the worse they seem to become), and to seek new health and security from a stable source outside of themselves. I make no apologies whatsoever for offering Christ as the only real answer. Through Christ, God can heal absolutely anything, and through Christ, we are able to see God and realise what he is really like.

When a person turns from their troubles to someone who is stronger, burdens are lifted and strength is gained. To be healthy we need firm security from outside ourselves – in trusting relationships. We need to know that there are those we can depend upon and love, and that we are needed and loved by them as well. The best kind of security lies in being able to surrender our independence and share our life with someone we can always trust. The best security of all lies in being able to surrender our independence and share our life with God, for only God's love, patience and strength are endless, and only he can always enable us to cope.

For many such a thought is far too inhibiting or threatening. They seek escape routes instead. We need to realise that we can never escape from ourselves – though so many people try to! To be whole, we must accept ourselves as we are, let ourselves go into the hands of God, and then allow him to make us everything that he wants us to be. Therein lies the healthy life, the life of fullness and wholeness.

This was the teaching of Jesus which was also part of his healing ministry in Galilee. Many of the problems and illnesses may be a bit different today, but his ways to healing and wholeness have not changed at all. He is still calling us to face up to life and not run away, to accept ourselves and trust in God to make us all that we can be, and to use all the strength, support and healing that God gives.

Stephen had suffered from regular bouts of depression for over twenty years, ever since he was sixteen. He felt unable to cope with his everyday responsibilities and things seemed to be getting worse and worse. What was even more frustrating was that no one at all ever seemed to notice his problem; no one cared and he just wanted to isolate himself from everyone and everything. He even contemplated suicide as a way out. When the heart-attack came and he found himself in hospital, at first he didn't care whether he got better or not. But then, with much time to think about his life, his worries and his future, he decided to try for a new start. He had been a casual Christian for a long time, but now he asked God to take over his life, to take care of his worries and to give him a new start. He came out of hospital shining with a new determination to make the most of his life, and somehow he knew that everything was going to be different. He found himself able to cope with his everyday responsibilities and times of depression were only occasional – when he dwelt on his troubles and kept them to himself. Since then he has only experienced one bout of heart trouble, which was at a particularly upsetting time emotionally. He still goes through times of difficulty, but finds that when those difficulties are shared with God he can begin to cope.

2. Barriers to Wholeness

Relationships

Having considered our needs and the ways that stress can affect health, we must now look briefly at some of the main barriers to wholeness and health. The first of these concerns our relationships.

Bad relationships can be blocks to healing and barriers to wholeness. Feelings of bitterness, hatred or jealousy towards others will always spoil our wholeness. Not only can such feelings cause illness and be blocks to healing, but also they may grow to dominate our lives and separate us from God. To be really whole we need to be in right relationships with God, with other people and also with ourselves!

Our wholeness can be spoiled by the effects of bad relationships both in the past and in the present. Our childhood relationships with our parents are vital in the growth of our personalities. We look to parents for all our needs of love, security and example. If those needs have not been met with care and tenderness, this is bound to make our adult relationships difficult, if not unhealthy, especially in marriage. Our childhood relationships towards parents and other dominant figures in our lives can be the cause of our growing up with feelings of inferiority, guilt, isolation or fears of others. Jealousy, resentment, anger and even hatred can easily result.

Our present relationships with partners, parents, children, neighbours and work-mates are likely to dominate both our outlook on life and our health. If we have grown up with feelings of bitterness and aggression, these are likely to affect not only our relationships with other people, but also our relationship with God. We are liable to feel resentful and angry with God too! It is so sad to see people clinging to such feelings, and unable to forgive. Lack of forgiveness is the greatest spoiler of relationships with others and with God. Only if we are prepared to let go of bitterness can its causes be healed by God.

How it hurts me when I encounter bitterness between members of our congregation. If it hurts *me* so, as pastor, how much more must it pain God as Father to watch as two of his children strive to hurt each other. The reasons for such frictions begin way back in the past, even though they have a present focus, but neither party would ever be likely to realise or admit this. The problem always seems to be with the other person! However, unless those involved are willing to forgive one another, as God forgives, they can never be whole.

Sometimes people tell me they will forgive, but not forget. Forgiveness with a 'but' or an 'if' is never wholehearted forgiveness. While it may be very difficult to forget others' hurts or wrongs, real forgiveness does involve overcoming these with love. It is only love that can enable us to let go completely of all bitterness and resentment and really forgive. Those who insist on clinging on to resentful or bitter feelings may well find that ill-health is the price they have to pay – and probably a fair bit of unpopularity too!

Negative Attitudes

A further significant barrier to wholeness can be negative attitudes. Many a possible healing – by medical or prayerful means – is blocked by the negative attitudes of the patient.

First of all there is the patient who doesn't want to get better. He tends to be a person who has become so used to living with his illness or disability (and the accompanying attention) that he just couldn't imagine life without it, although he would never admit to the fact and probably doesn't even realise it. He is rather like the long-term prisoner who, upon release, instinctively returns to careless crime. He cannot cope with life outside prison walls and so he seeks to return to the security of prison life without even realising it.

Secondly there is the person who allows sickness to rule without fighting back. This kind of negative attitude is most understandable amongst those with long-term or recurrent illnesses. Norman is much involved in the life and ministry of the church, and is usually a bright and cheerful figure. However, from time to time he suffers from bouts of arthritis which put him out of action for a little while. After a few days at home, the illness often begins to get the better of him; he finds it difficult to fight back and the illness seems to get worse. Then he often needs a bit of encouragement to get back on his feet again. But when he does fight back, and gets busy with his ministry, or his garden, the arthritis soon disappears again. Unless we fight sickness, it usually grows worse.

The third negative attitude is that of the person who sees no hope, who has given up and succumbed completely to his illness. He does not believe he can be cured, and that very fear or non-belief actually prevents any cure! I firmly believe that patients should always be made aware of the nature and extent of their illness, unless there is some medical reason for not doing so. The greatest fear is the unknown, and we cannot fight against what we do not know. A positive belief and a fighting spirit are known to be strong factors in combating all kinds of illness, including cancers. However, I do not believe that terms like incurable or no-hope should ever be used. Whilst an illness may appear medically incurable, many terminal conditions have been reversed through prayer. Nothing is ever definitely incurable to God. It is absolutely vital that we never take away a person's hope, for it may be that by clinging to a single slim hope a person is able to fight back and pull through. We must always have a positive, hopeful attitude towards sickness.

It is the task of the Christian minister to help to dispel negative attitudes towards sickness, and to help the sick person to fight back using all the resources that God gives. No matter how bleak a situation may appear, we must always bring hope.

Unholiness

A further barrier to health and wholeness can be unholiness or sinfulness. Sin is always an unpleasant and unpopular word, but it sums up all that is unholy, all that makes us turn away from God. Sometimes a person's unholiness can be the root of his illness, or may be the block to his healing. Sin creates barriers between us and God which can cut us off from his healing power. All that is unloving, unrighteous and unclean, that is sin! It is the unholy part of our life that we usually prefer to keep hidden from others, and its effects can be feelings of guilt, shame or rejection.

Jesus was well aware when sin was at the root of a person's trouble or illness, and forgiveness was the first step needed towards living a whole life.[6,7] Just as a child who is ashamed of something he has done needs the assurance of his parents' forgiveness and continued love, so too when we feel unholy we need to know that our loving Father will forgive us. How encouraging is the parable of the Lost (Prodigal) Son or the Forgiving Father as many prefer to call it.[8] The younger son returns home in shame and disgrace, to find the father waiting with open arms just longing to forgive him. Contrast this with the understandable jealousy of the elder son as his father's loving forgiveness is lavished upon his brother. Yet his own jealousy and unforgivingness is now separating *him* from his father's love! How often we too separate ourselves from God's love and forgiveness, because we just cannot forgive others.[9]

We need to be aware that when people express a sense of guilt, rejection or shame, there may well be a need to know forgiveness. We all do things we regret, and need opportunities to say we're sorry and receive forgiveness. It can be hard to say you're sorry sometimes, especially when pride is at stake, but repentance is the only sure way to forgiveness. It is not unusual for a person to want and need to share some secret sin in order to receive and know God's forgiveness. Because Christ has already paid the price for all of our wrongs, we can offer the assurance that forgiveness is there for all who really want it; there is no need for anyone to feel trapped in guilt or shame.

In considering Christ's healing ministry, I suppose few people would include stories of people like Zacchaeus the unscrupulous tax-collector. Yet Zacchaeus' unholiness made him a 'sick' person who had lost his way. His encounter with Jesus enabled him to be whole again.[10] This much-despised figure, whose swindling life was one of self-centredness and bad relationships, was made whole!

In Christian healing ministry we often over-emphasise outward physical healings. What goes on inside a person is even more important, and this usually affects physical health anyway. It is when people are healed inside that real changes can be seen in their outward lives, as happened to Zacchaeus.

3. Healing and Medicine

Causes of Sickness

It is generally accepted in the medical world that the majority of illnesses (some would say up to ninety per cent) have emotional causes. If people are to be made whole, then causes as well as the illnesses themselves must be dealt with. Even though an illness may appear to have been cured, if its root-cause remains then that person is not whole. In any concern for healing and wholeness we need to be aware of such emotional factors. We need to know a little about the connections between physical illness and our spiritual and emotional health.

Illnesses can have various causes, and physical problems can be the result of emotional disorders within a person. Let me give some examples: heart problems can have their source in anxieties or stress, particularly the concern to succeed or to do well; recurrent headaches can be the result of frustrations or worries; fear can sometimes be the cause of asthma, often when a person feels separated from the security of home and family; it is well known that stomach ulcers can be brought on by worries, and feelings of being unloved can also be a cause; a person who feels rejected or unwanted can sometimes suffer from epilepsy; colitis can occur as the result of an emotional crisis such as the death of someone close, and it is sometimes an alternative reaction of the body to depression; people who suffer from depression, whatever *its* cause may be, are always more open to infection than others; periods of acute shock or stress can lead to the occurrence of an over-active thyroid gland; severe shock can be the cause of many physical ailments including arthritis; and it is known that some forms of cancer can be brought on by shock or feelings of despair, often after bereavement. This list of possible causes of physical illness could go on and on, but I must emphasise that these are only *possible* causes amongst many.

In ministering to those who are physically ill, it can be very helpful to begin by going back over events during the two years or so before the illness became evident, to see whether the patient can recall any particularly traumatic time or experience. When they can, we are often able to find the source of the problem. This can be of help both to the patient and to the process of healing through prayer.

Repressed feelings frequently reveal themselves through physical disorders: various kinds of skin problems can be the result of repressed anger; repressed bitterness and an unwillingness to forgive can bring on arthritis; feelings of guilt may not only cause depression, but sometimes forms of paralysis; and all kinds of bodily pains can result from wrong intentions towards others. Such emotional disorders can be the source of a wide variety of physical ailments, but once again I must emphasise that these are only *possible* causes.

Sometimes, however, God heals without any human knowledge of the causes of a physical illness. On a number of occasions it has only been *after* a healing that I have realised the emotional cause. So *we* do not always have to know the causes. But then, on other occasions, it has been lack of knowledge of the cause that has either delayed or prevented healing. It is therefore well worth beginning by trying to isolate root-causes, and focussing our prayers there.

Responses to Sickness

There are various means of responding to illness – by medical treatment, through surgery, with counselling and with prayer for healing. These different ways of responding should never work in opposition to each other; they are complementary. Healing can come through any of these sources, or through a combination of several.

Sometimes people feel that to seek medical help is a sign of lack of faith. This is not so! Some doctors see Christian healing ministry as a threat of amateur interference. This is sad! All true healing comes from God, and he has given us all kinds of gifts, skills and resources with which we can become partners in the healing process. Together, we have so much more to offer the sick.

Phyllis believed she was suffering from a prolapse of the womb. She was upset and worried, but kept the problem to herself. However, she took the chance to attend a Roman Catholic healing meeting, and although she was not healed of the trouble, she returned home with a persistent message, that secret illness, kept to oneself, will always develop in the dark-room of fear, unless exposed to the light! She told her family, and then went to see her doctor. Following treatment and much prayer the situation had not improved and an operation seemed to be the only answer.

We prayed for her just before she went into hospital; she was admitted confident that she was in God's hands and that all would go well. On the night before her operation she was given her first ever sleeping tablet and slept very soundly. Next morning she still felt quite drowsy, and failed to notice the 'nil by mouth' sign hanging over her bed. By mistake she was given the breakfast of another patient with the same name. She really enjoyed her tea and toast! Just twenty minutes later the trolly arrived to take her down for her operation. That morning her daughter decided to come into church to pray for her. She was joined by another church member who had an inner feeling that something was wrong and that prayer was needed. It was five to nine as they knelt down together to pray. It was five to nine as Phyllis passed the clock on the way to the operating theatre, and felt a sudden urge to mention to the sister that she had had a nice breakfast. After the initial panic the operation was postponed. Had Phyllis had an anaesthetic, the consequences could have been fatal.

Two weeks later, without an early breakfast, Phyllis had her operation, a hysterectomy. Within twenty-four hours she was up and about; after two weeks she was at home and back to normal, a quite remarkably speedy recovery for anyone, let alone a woman of seventy! What a fine example of all the approaches and responses to sickness working hand in hand; counselling, treatment, surgery and prayer!

The more co-operation there is between the medical service and Christian healing ministry, the better for everyone. There can be many misunderstandings between doctors and those involved in Christian healing ministry, and how much better it would be for doctors, ministers and above all patients, if all could work in mutual harmony to bring healing and wholeness.

Curing, Healing and Wholeness

Curing illnesses is the task of gifted, trained and able human beings. Healing and bringing wholeness is the work of God. Doctors may be able to treat and cure, counsellors to pinpoint and advise, ministers to respond and pray – but only God can heal.

When a surgeon conducts an operation all may go well, with the offending problem removed or repaired, and he may make a marvellous job of everything. But then the healing must take place, and only God can effect this. When a doctor recommends suitable medical treatment, he may well have chosen the best antidote, but only God can ensure the healing. When a counsellor correctly discerns the source of a problem and sensitively guides his patient towards coping with it, he may well have done his patient a great service, but only God can actually heal. When a Christian ministers to a sick person, he may minister with deep love and pray with great faith, but only God has the power to heal. Man can care and cure, but only God can bring healing and wholeness.

Saul was a man of tremendous potential, but he was a tragically misguided figure, and his spiritual life was a mess! He was anything but whole. On the road to Damascus he encountered the light of Christ and was struck with blindness. He needed healing, but more than that he needed to be made whole, and the only way that could come about was by his surrender to Christ. Through Ananias he received healing; through Christ he was made whole again.[11]

Through the cross we are offered much more than healing; we are offered complete wholeness, fullness of life, new oneness with God. As Saul came to realise, the real way to wholeness involves surrender to Christ; the two go hand in hand.

It is God's will that we should not only be healthy, but whole. In Christian healing ministry, our goal must be more than just health; it must be wholeness. The way to both health and wholeness is by the surrender of ourselves to Christ, allowing him to take over our lives. When we are made whole, healing usually (though not always) follows, and lasts. Even if we are not physically healed at the time, at least we will receive and know the peace of God, to enable us to cope with and use our illness for good. Far better to be whole though not healed, than cured but not whole!

Notes

1. Mark 2:5
2. John 5:14
3. Mark 1:23-26
4. Matt. 8:28-34
5. e.g. Matt. 9:32-34 & 12:22-23
6. e.g. Mark 2:5
7. e.g. John 8:11
8. Luke 15:11-32
9. Matt. 18:21-35
10. Luke 19:1-10
11. Acts 9:1-20

Chapter 9

THE HEALING OF 'PRISONERS'

The Spirit of the Lord is upon me,
        because he has chosen me to bring good news to the
        poor.
He has sent me to proclaim liberty to the captives,
        and recovery of sight to the blind;
to set free the oppressed and announce that the time has
        come
        when the Lord will save his people

                                        (Luke 4:18-19 GNB).

1. Who are the 'Prisoners'?

When Jesus spoke the above words in the synagogue at
Nazareth, he was quoting prophetic words of Isaiah referring
to himself and his ministry. He was the one who had come
bearing good news for the poor, bringing release for prisoners, sight for the blind and freedom for the oppressed. We
do not hear of Christ's visiting any jails or places of extreme
repression, so we might wonder just who were these prisoners
and oppressed people, and when and how Jesus set them free.

The captives to whom Jesus came were those who were
prisoners of either their past experiences, their present situations or sometimes their fears for the future – and often
combinations of all these. Many were prisoners of physical
illness, and some of mental disorders; some were imprisoned
by their relationships, or the way others regarded them;
others were imprisoned by spirits of evil; many were slaves to
material things – money and possessions; while still others

were prisoners to fears and emotions. Jesus' whole ministry was one of setting people free; he was surrounded by crowds and individuals clamouring for release, and he travelled from place to place dealing with the many kinds of things that prevented people from living a life of wholeness, fullness and freedom.

Many of those to whom Jesus ministered might not immediately be recognised as having been prisoners. Apart from his many physical healings and exorcisms, we read of Jesus setting Peter free, imprisoned by feelings of past guilt and failure; ([1] & see below) the woman at the well, a prisoner of both her present circumstances and probably past feelings too;[2] the woman caught in adultery, imprisoned by the condemnation of others;[3] Zacchaeus, enslaved by his dependence upon money and material things;[4] and even Saul, imprisoned by indoctrination and hatred.[5] In fact, if we were to consider each person or group that Jesus encountered, then we would see that almost every one was a prisoner in some way or other. Time after time, Jesus revealed their prisons and then set free those who wished to be set free.

As we look around today, we find that the situation is still much the same; the world is full of prisoners. Besides those who are captives in a physical, political or geographical sense, we find there are countless prisoners of physical and mental illness, of disabilities and disadvantages, of fears and frustrations, habits and addiction, of money and other material things, of oppression or possession by evil spirits, of emotions and anxieties, bad relationships or a low self-image, and so the list could go on. In this chapter I want to look at some of the ways in which we can minister to those who are prisoners not so much of physical illness, but more of their past experiences, present circumstances or fears for the future.

Past Experiences

We are each moulded into the people we are by many factors. Besides hereditary influences, we are affected by our upbringing, in particular our relationships with parents, our experiences, especially those of childhood, our environment and education, and our many different relationships and encounters. It is in the early years of life, before the age of five, that most of the shaping of our characters and personalities takes place. During these formative years, children can easily be scarred permanently by bad experiences or relationships, which then affect their whole attitude to life in later years. For example, a bad relationship with a key figure can ruin our ability to make loving relationships in later life; a frightening experience can lead to permanent phobias; what parents tell us about ourselves and about life can become firmly fixed in our minds. If relationships, experiences and impressions as children are particularly negative in any way, then we become prisoners, prisoners of our past.

Norma spent all but eighteen months of her first nine years in hospital, having had tuberculosis of the spine. Hospital was her home. When she was well enough to return to her family, she felt out of place and unwanted; she was just another mouth to feed in a large family. For her it was like being an orphan. Although her father was kindly, she could never feel really close to mother, brothers or sisters. For Norma life at home involved countless hurtful experiences, especially in her relationship with her mother. She built around herself a tough protective shell and made herself as independent of others as she could. She would avoid getting close to people, for experience had taught her that this was a sure way to get herself hurt. She developed a deep and very personal relationship with God, but her life remained a life of loneliness. Norma had become a sad figure; she didn't believe that anyone could ever love her for who she was, except God. Often she would rush away alone for moments of crying and depression, but they were also moments when she could feel especially close to God.

As an adult, she had become very wary of trusting people and reluctant ever to receive anything from them. Unconsciously, she would often do things to draw attention to herself, so as not to feel inferior to others. The Norma people would see appeared to be strong, confident and outgoing; the real Norma was a very different person indeed.

As I grew to know Norma well, over a long time, I began to catch glimpses of the person she really was. Eventually, a little reluctantly, she was able to tell me about her childhood and upbringing, although it was an extremely hurtful and difficult task for her to go over again so many painful experiences. They were things that she had always kept hidden away in her inner memory because they were too painful even to think about. Yet they were the very experiences that were making her a prisoner in the present, as she was eventually able to see. It was hard for Norma to entrust these secret hurts to someone else; trusting had never come easily. As we talked on many occasions, and saw how these past hurts were affecting all of her present attitudes, relationships and intentions, time and again she would get hurt once more.

For Norma it had been a great risk to allow someone else to see her as she really was, and yet all of this was becoming a healing experience, for we would also pray away these hurts as Norma began to try to be herself. The most crucial moment she remembers was when I pointed out that I found the 'apparent' Norma a difficult person to get close to, yet I could really love the real Norma. For a long time she just couldn't come to terms with this. As she didn't really love herself, she found it hard to imagine anyone else loving her.

Much, though not all, of that hurtful past has now been healed. Day by day, Norma is learning to accept herself as she really is and to be herself. Sometimes she seems to be doing well, but then a crisis or a conflict will force her back into her shell for a little while. It is so hard for a person who has lived all her life in a dark prison to move from its security out into the open. Yet the very fact that she has allowed me to share with you these very experiences is a great testimony to the extent of her healing so far. I pray that in the near future she will be able to leave behind her past-prison for ever.

I have recounted Norma's story because in her life we can see so many of the ways in which early relationships and experiences can not only affect a person's character, but also make that person a prisoner. Often the only road towards God's full healing of such wounds and scars is by many hours of careful conversation and prayer together, over a long period.

Today, there are more and more people who have not had all the childhood love, attention and encouragement that they so much needed and wanted. As adults, they develop various means by which to continue to seek this love and attention that they missed out on as children, and they usually go about this in quite the wrong way. Most tend to be rather insular and apparently independent people, like Norma. Others will try to win affection by means such as embarrassing generosity, by moodiness – intended to black-mail – or by forever criticising and putting down other people. Shortly we will be looking more closely at the reasons for such reactions, and also at some of the ways of bringing healing.

Present Situations

Whilst past experiences can cause imprisonment, so too can a person's present circumstances or situation. Besides the imprisonment of sickness and suffering, we can also be confined by feelings such as guilt, grief, resentment, hatred, obsessions, addictions and many many more. Although many of these feelings are much affected by the past, some-times the main problem lies in the present and in our present circumstances.

Jean had heard about the St Mark's ministry of prayer for healing, and she asked if we could help her. Before coming to a service of prayer for healing, she called to see me to chat about the nature of her problems. Eighteen months previous-ly her first baby was born, a little boy named John. However, from the moment of his birth she had felt overwhelmed by a sense of inadequacy as a mother. She felt that she just couldn't fulfil all his needs, and she would become depressed because she believed that she ought to be able to. She also felt guilty about this, and about the boredom she experienced with much of what mothering entails. The demands of a toddler seemed to dominate everything, leaving little opportunity for adult conversation or even adult thoughts. She wondered if it was all just post-natal depression that was bringing on so many negative feelings and preventing her from functioning normally. Even in the happiest times, when John's demands were not overwhelming her, she still felt a deep sense of guilt because things were not always this way. She felt that her trouble was very much tied in with her personality, so she had not sought any help from her doctor. The feelings she had were recognised as those often present in her anyway, but magnified in her relationship with John.

As we talked together, we realised that Jean was very self-dependent and she agreed to prepare for coming to the service by beginning to rely on God a little more, and herself a little less. Some time after coming to a service of prayer for healing, she wrote to me:

I feel that the healing process began when we talked together, a few days before I came to the service. It was as if I began to feel relieved that something would be done about the problem, and not by me, as I felt powerless to do anything about it myself.

The service itself struck me as very ordinary in its extra-ordinariness! The congregation were very warm and welcoming and there seemed a quiet certainty that things would change.

For a couple of days afterwards everything seemed to be as usual, until one morning when my little boy came into the house for the nth time to have his hands washed (he kept changing his mind about what he wanted to play with), and I realised that I was not tense, or over-reacting as I would have done before. It was then that I knew I had been healed. It wasn't a feeling, it was a knowledge.

Since then, yes, I've got uptight and still have feelings of unworthiness as a mother, but never to the destructive extent of before the healing. Since then, I have been able to enjoy John in a way that I couldn't have done previously.

Jean's story echoes just one of many problems experienced by women who feel a certain sense of imprisonment in the home at times. Today, the frustration of unemployment has brought such domestic captivity to men too. Others experience imprisonment in their environment, their work, their relationships or their emotions and anxieties. Shortly we must look more closely at these too, and at how we can enable God to bring release.

Fears for the Future

Finally and more briefly, there are those who are overwhelmed by fears for the future. Although such fears cannot be separated from past and present, the main focus of imprisonment seems to be the future. Sometimes these are the general concerns about the fate of the world and its inhabitants, but more often it is a personal worry: 'What's going to become of *me*?'

Behind such concerns there usually lurks a fear of death or of being left alone, probably inherited from the past. Again, the road to healing will usually involve much counselling over a period of time, with prayer for healing and possibly laying on of hands.

2. Healing of the Memories

Much has been written on this matter by others with considerably more understanding and experience than I, and some of the books listed in appendix 2 go into this area in detail. I offer just a brief introduction to this form of healing, which covers a wide range of problems, in order that readers may be aware of the potential causes of many fears, anxieties and personality disorders which stem from past experiences, and of how we can help to bring healing.

Hurts of the Past

There are two kinds of past hurts that we must be aware about: those that a person knows of, and those that he does not. The latter are hurts tucked away in the dark corners of his mind, of which he is quite unconscious. But let us first consider the hurts that a person is all too conscious of.

Such hurts can include general childhood experience of which we are much aware, like lack of love, constant criticism or feelings of rejection. There are also others such as things we have been deprived of, the death of someone close or deep regrets about things in the past that we have either done or not done. All of these kinds of hurts can have lasting effects on both health and personality.

Paul suffered from a form of nervous colitis. Frequently he found himself enduring a most unpleasant and uncomfortable day, with the embarrassment of being unable to stray far from a toilet. He had realised that these bouts usually occurred either after an upsetting experience or after eating certain foods such as fruit and vegetables, cereals and beer. His doctor had given Paul various tranquillisers and diarrhoea tablets, which helped a little, and he had slowly grown to live with his problem by avoiding these particular foods and any tense situations, if he could. The illness had begun seven years earlier, shortly after the death of his six-year-old daughter, and Paul was aware that his illness was probably connected with the deep hurt of this experience.

Although Paul became much involved in prayer for the healing of others, he never actually got around to asking God to heal *him*, as he had learned to live with his problem. Eventually he and his wife agreed to become church leaders and were commissioned at a midweek service of prayer for healing. As Paul was being commissioned, his wife also prayed for his healing. Paul himself made a recommitment of his whole self to God's service, experiencing a great sense of excitement at the time, but he never gave a thought to his need for healing.

A few weeks later, his wife (whom I shall not call Eve !) tempted him to eat a small piece of orange. Although he realised that this for him was one of the 'forbidden fruits' as far as his illness was concerned, he ate it as he so enjoyed oranges. He was surprised that this had no effect on his system, and decided to try again the next day, this time taking two pieces. The following day it was three, and steadily he began to try all the various foods that were on the doctor's forbidden list – all with no effect. His wife then told him of how she had prayed for his healing, and together they were able to thank God for his response. Paul has had no such trouble since.

With these kinds of past hurts it is usually necessary for someone else to point out the link between the hurt and the physical illness or personality problem, before praying for healing. In Paul's situation, he was well aware of the link himself, and God simply took over as requested when Paul made his commitment and his wife prayed for his healing.

In ministering to those with such past hurts, it is helpful to begin by making them aware that the cause of the present problem lies in the past. That done, it will then take careful and sensitive enquiry, to enable the person to go over such hurts again, in order to find together the root-cause of the present problem. It is then most appropriate to pray, with laying on of hands, for Christ to come and heal these hurts, and to sort out the present problems they have caused.

'Dark Corners'

The other type of past hurt which can have a great effect on our lives is a hurt that our conscious mind has completely forgotten. It is usually focussed on a single incident which has become shut away in the dark corners of our mind and which is just too painful or too frightening to remember. Such unexposed hurts can be the causes of various recurrent problems, rendering a person a prisoner of a forgotten experience.

For example, an experience of severe shock at some time can bring on loss of speech, hearing or even sight; a childhood experience of being locked in a cupboard can be a cause of claustrophobia, or the extremely common fear of lifts; even a forgotten experience as a baby can cause a lasting fear or phobia. I have a friend who has an irrational fear of butterflies; she will scream at the sight of even a picture of one. I am sure that this fear stems from a frightening encounter with a butterfly as a baby.

In order to bring healing from the effects of such an experience, it is usually necessary to discern the root of the problem – the hidden experience itself – and this is never easy. *We* have not the perception or insight necessary to explore the unconscious mind, but *God* has! We must therefore learn to minister by complete reliance upon the guidance of God's Holy Spirit, through prayer.

Perhaps at this point you may feel that we are going too deep, and that you would rather leave this kind of ministry to the professionals. I too have felt this way, yet over a period of time I have been learning to pray alongside others in this new way, by relying all the time upon God's guidance through his Holy Spirit. Even in counselling situations, whilst listening to another person, I can pray for the Holy Spirit's discernment of the root problem. It is because I know that I am out of my depth and unable to proceed on my own, that I have no choice but to rely upon the guidance of the Holy Spirit. Unlike some others, I have not found that this guidance comes through visions or striking revelations. It comes either through the other person's being able to remember the key incident, or through some strong thought coming into my mind which I know is not my own, and which directs to the source of the problem. Usually this has turned out to be a painful incident from childhood days: the specific occasion when a daughter felt most acutely her father's constant condemnation and rejection; the winter night when a young girl felt desperate fear, as she was sent alone, in the dark, to her distant bedroom at the far side of a large house; the agonising moment of a young boy, an only child, when he overheard his mother declare, during a parental argument, that she had never wanted a child in the first place.

When two people pray together for the Holy Spirit's guidance as to the hidden hurt at the root of a problem, then by patience in prayer he is able to guide. He may reveal this to either person or lead one to 'spark' the other concerning the source of the problem. At this point it is then necessary to ask Christ to come into that situation with his healing, forgiveness, peace or whatever else is needed.

Ruth Carter Stapleton recommends a form of healing meditation which involves enabling a person to relive prayerfully the experience, this time bringing Christ into the situation to recreate it in a new and healing way.[6] Others have found this method most helpful. For my own part, I have not found it so; sometimes I have found that people just cannot recreate the situation in their minds with Jesus present, and on other occasions I have felt that people have just been 'playing along' with me. I have found it most helpful to simply ask Christ to heal the effects of the incident or experience. This kind of prayer is often known as prayer for inner healing.

Our Self-image

It is from the relationships of our childhood years, especially with our parents, that we gain our self-image. If, as children, we have been constantly praised and favourably compared with others, then we develop a high opinion of ourselves, and may well become conceited and unpopular. If, on the other hand, we were forever being criticised and made to feel useless and a failure, then it will hardly be surprising if, as adults, we display a lack of self-confidence and have a weak self-image. A child who is always being told how wicked he is is liable either to grow up wicked or with a guilt-problem, while another who is constantly made to feel a nuisance will probably become apologetic, always sensing that he is in the way.

Arthur had suffered from migraines since he was a teenager. He had had a particularly insecure childhood, with little experience of parental love, and was greatly lacking in self-confidence, for he had always been made to feel backward and a failure in life.

I had been calling on Arthur for some time, to talk through many of these past hurts in order to begin to build up his self-confidence, and to help him realise that he was both acceptable and lovable as his real self. (He had built up a very different public image in order to conceal his true feelings about himself). Healing was beginning to come, through our conversations and prayers together, but I had not been aware of his migraine problem. Apparently these occurred mostly when he did something different from usual: a holiday, an outing, a party or some special responsibility. They would cause sickness too, eventually forcing him to bed, and they could last for several days, with tablets offering little relief.

At one of our Sunday evening services he came forward for prayer with laying on of hands on behalf of a close friend. As we prayed with him, he experienced something like an electric shock passing through his body. Some weeks later, he realised that he was no longer having the migraines or needing to use his tablets. I believe that Arthur's healing came about both through the prayers in church and the conversations and prayers that we had been sharing in his home.

When a person has developed a negative self-image, this needs to be gently pointed out and prayed about. As that person begins to talk about parents and childhood days, the reasons why this has arisen should quickly emerge. It is then necessary to point out that this self-image is not in fact a real one, but has been created by others, and then to pray for healing.

3. Healing of Negative Perspectives

Loving Others as We Love Ourselves

When Jesus commanded that we should love our neighbours as we love ourselves,[7] I believe that he chose his words carefully. Although this command is so often quoted as an injunction to love others, there is rarely mention made of the fact that we are also called to love ourselves. Whilst Jesus was not advocating a 'look after number one' attitude to life, he was pointing out that we need to be able to love and accept ourselves as we really are in order to really love others. People who grow up feeling unloved and unacceptable tend to come to view themselves as unlovable and sometimes rather worthless. Such people will use many means to try to love and spoil themselves: compulsive spending, over-eating and other forms of self-indulgence; they are usually very critical of others, though particularly sensitive to any criticisms of themselves. Their life can soon become a fruitless search for love, a love which they cannot really conceive of.

In day to day life, I have come across many people who do not love themselves. Furthermore, they feel that because God knows them as they really are, he could not love them either. It is not surprising that they have relationship difficulties with others too, usually tending to complain that others do not like them, which is a logical assumption if you don't really like yourself! Much prayerful counselling is necessary to set things right again.

It is important that the counsellor first expresses and shows that 'God loves (the real) you', and 'I love (the real) you, too'. Feelings of rejection can only be countered by evidence of acceptance not just by others, but first of all by the person involved in counselling, who may also point to himself as evidence of God's love. Besides the evidence of God's love through Christ's ministry and sacrifice, a person needs first to be sure that the counsellor loves and cares for him, in order that a trusting relationship may be established.

Next it is vital that a person begins to face up to who he

really is. He needs to realise that God has created no one as useless, worthless or unacceptable. Wrong images need to be shown up for what they are, by examining how they were originally gained in childhood. Once a person realises that he is truly loved and accepted by God, and that God longs to achieve so much through his life, he can begin to rely on God's strength instead of forever focussing on his own weaknesses. Until a person has begun to love and accept himself, it is useless to try to sort out consequent problems such as bad relationships, over-indulgence or even addictions.

Those who have difficulty loving themselves always seem to have even more difficulty in giving love to and receiving love from others. Quarrels and differences tend to be quite frequent.

In a bad relationship with someone else, we all tend to focus on what is wrong with *them* and upon what *they* have done wrong. This is negative thinking, designed to prolong differences. The bad relationships that *we* feel result from things that are wrong in *us*; feelings of inadequacy or points of sensitivity through past hurts. While Jesus hated much of what he saw going on in the minds, actions and lives of those around him, he never hated people themselves. He was sometimes very angry, often deeply sad, and although he was put through absolute agony by others, he still managed to love and forgive them; he just hated what they were doing. *We* may rightly hate the things that others say about us or do to us, but if we bear them ill will, then it is *we* who have a problem, a 'love problem', which probably goes back to childhood days and experiences.

Whenever I encounter bitterness in people – which is far more often than I would wish – I am not initially concerned to sort out the matter of present focus, or to demand apologies and forgiveness. It is first important to seek out the past hurts which have brought these feelings to the surface in that person's life. Only when the reasons for this reaction have become clear is a person able to realise just how misguided and misdirected such feelings are. We are all liable to use others as scapegoats in revenge for childhood hurts!

The process of healing negative perspectives concerning love usually comes through prayerful counselling in the ways already outlined, though we must realise that sometimes it can come through God's direct intervention, or through other forms of counselling.

Loneliness and Grief

Those who feel unloved also tend to experience desperate loneliness in their lives. When chatting with those who are lonely, I often find that they seem to have been lonely for all or most of their lives. Sometimes a strong and loving marriage relationship can alleviate the loneliness, but if the marriage partner should die then back comes all the loneliness with the overwhelming grief of bereavement.

Within our church fellowship we have (or should have) a powerful means of helping the lonely to feel loved and wanted not only by us, but also by God. True knowledge of God's love, backed up by the loving care of the local church, can dispel loneliness forever. When Christians go out of their way to care for the lonely with gentleness and sensitivity, then healing comes naturally.

This was Jenny's experience. She lived alone, had no close friends and had been deeply hurt by the deaths of both her mother and her husband. She felt that there was now no one to love her, particularly as she had very little contact with the rest of her family. A neighbour had invited her to come along to church. She began to enjoy the fellowship and atmosphere, but still she felt lonely. Then she came to a midweek service of prayer for healing, and it was at the moment when another member of the congregation spontaneously gave her a great hug that she was healed. She had been rather taken aback really, but the experience of loving touch was something she had not known for a long time, and it brought with it a deep inner healing of all her feelings of hurt and loneliness. She actually felt love penetrating 'where nothing else had been able to reach', and with it came a deep sense of peace. Since that day, not only has her personality changed and developed quite dramatically, but also she is so much more confident and out-going.

Guilt

There are two main sources of guilt feelings: the first is the guilt we feel as a result of something we have done wrong, or something we should have done that we haven't; the second is the guilt feeling that can be inherited from childhood, but which is not actually the result of any wrong-doing.

When a person has done wrong it is right that he should feel regret and the need to know forgiveness. Otherwise feelings of guilt can begin to prey on his mind, making him a prisoner, and can even become such a dominant factor in his life that physical illness results.

Many believe that when Jesus asked Peter three times whether he loved him, beside Lake Tiberias, he was in fact healing Peter of his feelings of guilt and shame because of the three times he had denied Christ in Jerusalem.[1] He needed the opportunity to affirm his love, to know Jesus' forgiveness, and to receive a 're-commissioning'. These are good guidelines to follow when ministering to those who feel this kind of guilt.

The second kind of guilt usually stems from childhood days. When parents have been constantly critical of a child, he will develop a sense of being a failure. If this is pressed further he may also develop a sense of guilt both at what he has failed to do and what he has not done well. Such guilt feelings are not uncommon and tend to lead to depression and a hopeless striving to do things to perfection. It can also cause a totally unbalanced image of God, as the ever-critical judge who is watching closely to condemn us each time a foot is put wrong!

This was the image of God that Edna had (see p. 37). As a child she was made acutely aware of her own faults and failings, and religion was 'rammed down her throat'. Her father seems to have had a rather Victorian attitude to family life; he was quite feared by Edna, constantly critical of her, and ever warning of God's judgement upon all her failings. These feelings are so deeply ingrained into her ways of thinking and living that even after many hours of counselling she still cannot see that God wants her to accept his love, and wants to build her up rather than to destroy her by criticism. For Edna, the image of God as Father makes for comparisons with her own father. As soon as we pray, 'Our Father . . .' her picture of God as stern judge is reinforced, and she feels guilty again.

However, more often it is not nearly so difficult to bring healing and freedom from guilt. Sometimes it is sufficient just to find and expose the childhood source of the guilt feelings. At other times, prayerful healing of the memories is necessary too.

4. The Ministry of Deliverance

Oppression and Possession

Part of Christ's healing ministry involved conflict with evil spirits or demons which had taken a hold on people's lives, often causing mental or physical illness. Many choose to ignore or try to explain away this part of his ministry. However, it needs to be taken very seriously, for problems of oppression and possession by evil spirits are still much evident today.

Sometimes, when ministering to those who are clearly prisoners in one way or another, we can begin to realise that the problem is neither emotional, nor entirely due to past hurts. It may seem that there is a separate force or influence at work, over which the person has no control. This is known as 'demonic activity', and it calls for the ministry of deliverance. It is one of the most complex areas of Christian healing ministry, and those who minister need to proceed with caution.

This kind of activity becomes evident in three main ways:

the presence of evil spirits in homes or other places; the presence of evil spirits which annoy and oppress particular people (this I will refer to as oppression); and the presence of evil spirits which have actually entered into the mind and body of a person (this I will refer to as possession, although this does not necessarily mean that a person has been taken over entirely, for this is very rare indeed).

I have found the problem of evil spirits being present in houses to be surprisingly common. When I am called in to such a situation, I simply visit the home to pray in each room, commanding the departure of any evil presence in the name of Jesus Christ, and pray that Christ will himself fill the home with *his* presence instead. Problems of personal oppression usually come to light when a person complains about sensing pressure from an outside influence in his life, causing fear and depression. Forms of possession are less common, and more difficult to recognise. When a person has failed to respond to all other treatment, shows an uncontrollable compulsion to do wrong, is deeply depressed, usually to the extent of thinking in terms of suicide, and possibly hearing inner voices, then the possibility of possession must be considered.

Dangers and Warnings

I have used this heading as we begin to consider how to deal with these problems of demonic activity in order to emphasise the care and caution that needs to be taken. I have been very grateful to Revd John Banner for much help and guidance in this ministry, some of which I now offer here:

1. We must always try to avoid working alone. At least two people should always be involved. One may be in church praying while the other visits a troubled home, but it is best for a group of persons who are aware of such problems to be available as needed. The more serious the problem, the wider should be the prayer-circle of Christians involved.

2. We should prepare by praying-through Ephesians 6: 10-18, mentally putting on the whole armour of God

and praying for Christ's protection. We must always remember that we are ministering in the name and power of Jesus Christ, and under his protection. He has already gained complete victory over evil, and evil spirits or demons must bow to his command, just as they did in New Testament times.

3. We should pray for discernment of the full nature of the problem, seeking the guidance of the Holy Spirit, and we must proceed at all times with prayer and care.

4. We should use commands *in the name of Jesus Christ* rather than prayers of petition, and always act with the authority of Christ, as his representatives. For this kind of ministry we need confidence in Christ's authority, and not self-confidence!

When I first found myself drawn reluctantly into this area of ministry, I felt very weak and frightened, both because of my lack of understanding and my lack of dependence upon Christ. When first I visited a home with an evil presence, I prayed as I had been shown, but with little confidence – yet the problem disappeared! Since then I have been called to pray in many such houses, my confidence in Christ's effectiveness through prayer and obedience has grown tremendously, and on every occasion the house has been cleansed of its unwelcome guests.

When I am approached to visit such a house, I find that people begin to speak about the problem cautiously, testing my reactions, and will often just ask me to come and bless the house. They may speak of shadows moving, of eerie feelings of coldness, of animals going frantic, of furniture or ornaments moving about, of doors opening and closing or locking themselves, of strange sounds and of ominous footsteps. On two occasions, following bereavement, the widows have approached me to complain of spirits getting into bed with them, evil spirits which they were well aware were not the spirits of their dead husbands. I usually try to take someone with me on each occasion and to call in the daytime. Having followed beforehand the lines of preparation already outlined, I then pray – with the occupants – in *every* room of the house, commanding *in the name of Jesus Christ* that any presence of evil must depart to the place where it belongs never to return. Finally I pronounce God's blessing on the whole house and upon each of the occupants. I have always found this method to be effective, and have only rarely myself sensed any demonic activity whilst I have been present.

However, on one occasion I encountered a rather unusual situation. I was called to a house where a woman complained of what she believed was the presence of a man who once loved her and had subsequently committed suicide. We proceeded to move through the rooms of the house in the manner outlined, and eventually reached the last room, a dark bedroom. As I commanded the departure of any evil presence, the woman screamed out that she could no longer see. I prayed for the return of her sight, and it came back immediately. A few days later she phoned me to let me know that the trouble in the house had now gone, but that every time she went outside the spirit was waiting for her and would not leave her alone until she returned inside. I had wrongly diagnosed the full extent of the problem. It turned out to be a case of personal oppression, and we had to take her to church at a later date to deal with the problem.

In situations where we believe a person to be oppressed, this will usually have come to light through the person's own awareness. If, however, this has not been so, then the possibility of oppression should be talked over with great care and sensitivity; we never know quite how a person might react. It would be best to begin by enquiring about feelings of outside influence or pressure (without leading!), rather than by talking initially of spirits or demons. When the person is aware of the nature of the problem, he needs also to be made aware that the only way that it can be relieved is by his trusting in the power and love of the risen Christ. Unless he is prepared to proceed on these terms, with full co-operation and commitment in the manner I recommend, I am not prepared to go any further. This may sound as if I am being awkward or dogmatic, but I do this so that the person trusts

Christ rather than me, for only he can help, and so that the person involved does not begin to try to dictate the terms of healing. If he is not prepared to put his hand in the hand of Christ at this time, there is no point in proceeding anyway.

Madeleine asked for this ministry, and we invited her to come along to church early one evening. Beforehand the church elders met and prayed together along the lines already mentioned, and continued to pray as I went in the car to collect her. When she arrived in the room with us, she claimed that the spirit of oppression had not come into the room with her but was outside. We began by praying in the name of Christ that the spirit be bound and unable to harm Madeleine or anyone else. Then Madeleine was invited to confess her past involvement with evil, and to proclaim her new trust in Christ, with careful leading. The evil spirit was then commanded to depart from her, in the name of Christ, and to go to the place where it belonged. Finally, we laid hands on her to thank God for her healing. After our little prayer meeting, she seemed much more happy and relaxed until it was time to leave. Then she stepped outside with hesitancy, as if she expected someone to jump out on her. She looked around, declared with some surprise, 'He's gone!' and then relaxed and went home.

It is always important to advise a person who has been relieved of oppression that they must walk on in life trusting in Christ, and not become involved in any kind of evil. Sadly, Madeleine did not take that advice and is now experiencing further problems. She is not prepared to accept the terms I suggest for dealing with her troubles, so we are now unable to help her any further.

In cases where a person appears to be possessed by evil spirits, we must proceed with the greatest caution. If we have not had some worthwhile experience in this ministry, then it is vital to seek guidance from someone who has, possibly inviting him to lead you in this ministry at first. It is important too that a Christian doctor should be involved, for medical assistance may well be needed. I therefore offer no further advice here in this matter, except to point to the

guidelines outlined in *Wholeness and Healing*, the report of the
Bishop of Liverpool's Panel on the Ministry of Healing,
which are most helpful (see appendix 2).

A Healthy Approach

Those who become involved in Christian healing ministry
are likely to encounter these phenomena sooner or later. This
is not an area of ministry to be frightened of or to avoid. It
highlights our entire dependence upon Christ in healing
ministry, and this is good. We need to know how to respond
to situations of demonic activity, so that we are well prepared
to cope when they arise.

However, it is unhealthy to go about looking for demons
everywhere, or to develop too much interest in their activi-
ties. Some have a tendency to attribute all kinds of mental
and physical illness to demonic activity, and to seek con-
frontation. This was not Christ's way; he responded to those
who *came to him*.

Unless there seems good reason for considering the
involvement of demonic activity in a person's illness or
problem, then we should begin by using the methods of
responding to problems of an emotional nature which have
already been outlined. If then there has been little or no
improvement, and some of the warning signs already mentioned have become evident, it may be right to consider the
possibility of oppression or even possession. It can be helpful
to question the person about any past involvement in evil
practices such as séances or Ouija, or contact with people
involved in satanism or witchcraft, for such problems are
usually (but not always) caused by the person's own folly in
this way. If we are on the right track, something will usually
come to light at this point. To test for possession, the reading
of Revelation 20: 1-10 in the presence of the troubled person
is known to produce evidence of the presence of evil spirits
within a person by sharp reaction. Again, this test must be
used with carefulness and common sense.

Finally, a reminder about pastoral after-care. Once the

threat of evil spirits has been removed and 'the house swept clean', it is vital that the person remains holy and clean and trusting in Christ, avoiding any contact with evil. Jesus himself warned of the dangers of not doing so.[8] It is the Church's task to make sure that the person is cared for in this.

5. Prayerful Counselling

Today, Jesus longs to continue to set free the many who are prisoners, through the ministry of his Church. The prisons I have been describing are always places of darkness and despair, where no light has been allowed to shine, usually for some time past. They are places of anxiety, fear and depression in which people feel trapped and unable to set themselves free again. Sometimes they are dark and painful corners of past life, sometimes dark clouds of the present, but always they are hidden bonds that prevent a person from being whole and free.

It is the task of today's Church to bring into such prisons the love of Christ, to flood them with his marvellous light, exposing all bonds for the deceptions that they are. Jesus has given us the keys to unlock all the doors of these prisons, as we go in to share the hurts and tears of the prisoners, to respond with his love and care and to bring healing and freedom. He personally longs to lead all prisoners into real freedom, the freedom that no one else can ever offer, the freedom to experience and enjoy life in all its fullness. It is the task of his church to lead prisoners out of their prisons and into the love and care of Christ.

Responding to the 'Prisoner'

This part of Christ's healing ministry is bound to require of us much love and prayer and time. In our twentieth-century world of stress and strain, those involved in the caring professions are in great demand, and many feel most acutely the pressures of shortage of time. City doctors in particular can often find themselves under such pressure of time that tablets have to be prescribed as a second best to hours of counselling. In city life few people seem to have time to listen, and the support of the old family networks has almost disappeared, so that tranquillisers and anti-depressants have come to replace the sensitive listener. Yet such tablets rarely cure or heal – they simply push away problems for a few hours of respite before they return again – probably worse than before. Soon people can come to depend upon tablets to cope with life. Rather than becoming wrongly dependent on drugs, and enslaved to them, how much better to become dependent on Christ, who can set us free!

Thus it is our task as Christ's Church to come alongside the prisoners, and to lead them out to freedom. Whilst there are many skills that can be acquired for this work, and which are clearly vital in working with those with the most serious problems, we must not be put off at our own limited knowledge and understanding. What is far more important than knowledge and understanding is the willingness to listen, to care and to pray. We need to enter into others' problems and prisons, and then not just to sympathise, but to empathise in really feeling the pains that they feel. I am never ashamed or embarrassed by the fact that tears quite often come into my own eyes as I see and share the hurts of others. I believe that it is vital that we respond naturally – without trying to hide *our* feelings – as others share *their* deepest feelings. Such listening may be all that is needed to bring healing!

Unless we are prepared first to listen with care and understanding, then anything we say will be useless. Lots of clever, prepared guidance is much less likely to be of help, and we must remember that it is always more important to listen than to speak. We are not there to create an impression, but to show love! That love involves setting aside inhibitions and being natural. We should not sit apart from the other person, nor be hesitant in taking hold of a hand at moments of painfulness or for periods of prayer, and sometimes a gentle hug as we leave can say clearly what we feel in our hearts, and can also mean the world to the other person. The only hesitancy we need to have in this is the realisation of the danger of such actions being misinterpreted by someone of similar age and of the opposite sex!

So it is our primary task to respond to the prisoner with love and care, by sensitive listening, in order that we really may begin to feel what he feels and to share his burdens.

Responding to God

In seeking to respond to the prisoner, we must also seek to respond to God. In such counselling situations, we become the link-man between the other person and God. We are not called to become amateur psychologists or psychiatrists, for if we try to be clever we will surely make a mess of things. It is therefore vital that we make ourselves entirely dependent upon God, and ready to respond to the guidance of his Holy Spirit.

We do this by preparing in prayer beforehand, and also by praying through our meetings with the other person. If he is a Christian, much of this can be shared in open prayer together, but if he is not, then the quiet natural prayers of our minds will ensure that we are making a two-way response – both to the person and to God. In this way God is able to control the situation, and to guide us to the roots of a problem in his loving, Fatherly way. (We must also take careful note of the findings and opinions of others – doctors, psychiatrists etc. – for God can use all of us to reach the source of a problem.)

It is especially important that we should be responding to God, as a person leads us into the most painful areas of his past. He may well be doing this for the first time in his life, without thinking out the consequences. It is important to ask God (quietly) to give him peace about such opening up, for I have known some to feel very angry with me upon realising the risk they have taken in sharing such deep secrets. (This reminds me of the absolutely crucial need for complete confidentiality about anything that is shared. One careless word breaks the bond of trust and can leave the other person in a far worse situation than ever before.)

We also need to be willing to challenge when we perceive wrong views or interpretations of a situation. Again we will need to ask God (quietly) to enable the other person to accept such a challenge in the spirit in which it is intended. There are other ways too in which we need God's constant support throughout such conversations. Sometimes I find myself quite lost as to what to say or do next. An 'arrow prayer' is my way of asking God to guide us onward. At other times I find that I have to go away and pray about a situation for up to a week before being able to sense God's guidance. It is in such ways that we can enable God to control such counselling situations, beaming his light into the darkest corners, and then leading us out into his glorious sunshine.

Praying for Healing

There are then various ways of praying for healing. I will illustrate some through the stories of Colin, Valerie and Margaret.

Colin was one of the most tense and nervy people I had ever met. His life seemed to lead from one crisis to another, he always spoke quickly, and always of the latest upset. And yet he just couldn't cope with crises; he would panic, act rashly, and usually lose his temper. One day I commented on this to him and asked if he would like to come around for a chat to see if we could find out why his life continued in such a frantic manner. He gladly agreed and we arranged to meet weekly for a time.

Colin was a Christian, so on the first meeting we were able to begin by praying together that God would guide and control everything, and enable us to see the root-causes of all this tension. I had already noticed that Colin became most tense when he spoke of his mother, so we began to talk of his childhood and especially of his relationship with her. His mother had been the dominant figure in his home life, and although he had been well cared for, he had never felt really loved by her. His brother was always the favourite, and whatever he did and however hard he tried to please his mother, he had never felt able to succeed in doing so. A number of very painful experiences came to light which had apparently been long forgotten but which in fact were stored away in Colin's unconscious mind and were much affecting his present life. Through all of this, Colin had built up an image of himself as being unloved, un-needed and very much a failure. However, when we looked together at his life as it really was, he began to realise the falsity of this image of himself. He is very much a loved and needed person and nothing of a failure at all. At one stage in our conversations he was able to write down many of the reasons for his former image of himself, and then to cross out each factor as it was seen to be mistaken.

As many hurts were uncovered, and many feelings accounted for and then replaced by truth, there was much need for prayer together. Each week we would close our meeting with a time of prayer for healing of hurts, wrong impressions and bitter feelings, usually with laying on of hands. As the past was slowly healed, we then had to begin to look at the present. Colin had become quite a hard person, especially in his relationship with his mother, and we realised that above all else he was still striving in vain to please her and to become the favourite. His daily tension was caused by suppressed anger and frustration, and we realised that the time was shortly coming when he would have to go to see his mother, to begin to express and resolve his feelings, and then to forgive.

All of these factors had to be revealed by the guidance of God's Holy Spirit, for I have little training in counselling, and so it was vital that all of our conversations took place in a context of prayer. Finally, we believed that it was right for Colin to come forward at one of our Sunday services to receive prayers for healing with laying on of hands, before he set out to live with his new self-image, with his new tasks to complete and his new trust in God. This he did, with some nervousness. He is now considerably calmer and much more confident – most of the time – and is working on building up a new relationship with his mother.

Valerie is one of St Mark's lively teenage members. When she was in her mid-teens she began to have regular bouts of fainting. She would faint at home, at school, in church, and she would have to be careful as to where she went and what she did. Visits to the baths, which she so much enjoyed, were forbidden and she began to feel imprisoned by her condition and very worried about it. The doctors were unable to find the cause; blood tests, head scans, and heart tests only revealed a slight irregularity of heartbeat which would not be the cause, and no reason or cure could be found.

When the trouble reached its peak, Valerie was away from school for four months. She would faint without warning – sometimes up to ten times a day – and when she came to she would find herself quite unable to get up again without assistance; her body just wouldn't respond. She became frightened of falling over, ever-tired and sleeping for hours at a time during the day, and very depressed about the whole situation. She had been attending a clinic, where her trouble was attributed to a mild form of epilepsy, and appropriate tablets were prescribed. These helped, she was able to return to school, but still she would faint every few days.

We had been praying for Valerie for eighteen months when, one morning, I was given the understanding that her illness was psychosomatic and brought about by a difficult relationship with someone else. Although I knew this was of God's guiding (because I didn't really know what psychosomatic meant – I had to look it up!), I felt very reluctant to interfere. Who was I to make pronouncements when the doctors could not get to the root of the problem? I shared all of these feelings with my wife, who simply pointed out that if God was telling me to do something about the situation, then I had better do it! With some hesitation I went round to see Valerie to explain what I believed was the nature and cause of her trouble. This seemed to be confirmed when we were able to trace the start of her fainting to the time when this difficult relationship was at its worst. She agreed to come to the next service of prayer for healing, which was the first we had in the church itself.

She came to the service believing firmly that she was going to be healed, and backed up by the prayers of her family. When she came forward to receive prayers for healing with the laying on of hands, she experienced a feeling of special closeness to God, and she knew that he had healed her. The fainting ceased, she was able to give up her tablets and she has not been troubled with fainting since.

Margaret was due to fly to Canada for a holiday, but was absolutely terrified at the prospect of flying for the first time in her life, so much so that she began to question whether or not she would be able to go. Her worry about this had grown and grown. She came to a service of prayer for healing to ask for peace about the matter. When the time came for her to fly to Canada, she felt no fear at all and was able to board the plane in the confident trust that God was looking after her.

Notes

1. John 21:15-17
2. John 4:1-42
3. John 8:1-11
4. Luke 19:1-10
5. Acts 9:1
6. see appendix 2: *The Gift of Inner Healing* by Ruth Carter Stapleton.
7. Mark 12:31
8. Luke 11:24-26

Chapter 10

WHEN SOME ARE NOT HEALED

'I brought him to your disciples, but they could not heal him' (Matt. 17:16 GNB).

1. Coming to Terms with Non-healings

Facing Failure!

Jesus' disciples had become accustomed to healing and driving out evil spirits without difficulty. But then they are confronted by an epileptic boy with an evil spirit, they find that they cannot heal him and Jesus is not with them! Later, when Jesus himself has come to heal the boy, the disciples ask him why they could not heal him. Jesus answers that they have not enough faith, not enough trust in God.[1] In Mark's account of the incident, Jesus tells his disciples that only prayer can drive out this kind of spirit, again emphasising the need for complete dependence upon God.[2] Only Jesus himself seemed to have the oneness with God to heal in this instance.

In our ministry of prayer for healing, there are going to be those who are not healed. Even though we may pray in faith, and see many great and miraculous healings, there will still be some who are not healed as we expect. As I began to collect information and stories for this book, I appealed for details of both healings and non-healings that members of our congregation had experienced. Soon I had collected

many accounts of healings, some of which I had not previously been aware of, but I received little information about
non-healings. I appealed again – this time particularly for
non-healings – but still very few were able to help. Whilst I
am aware that people are much less likely to be keen to talk
about not having been healed, it is clear that many more have
been healed than not. However, I do know of quite a number
who have not been healed – mostly of more serious illnesses – and there have been times when I have found this
very difficult to accept. And yet, I can still usually see ways
that God has been at work, even though things may not have
turned out as we have wished or expected.

Pamela had looked after her father-in-law through serious
illness for two years before he died. Then she suffered a
heart-attack herself. Although she recovered from that, she
was left a pale shadow of her previous self. She suffered from
angina, her movements became very slow and sluggish, she
suffered from depression, and she lost her confidence to such
an extent that she became reluctant to remain on her own
indoors, and quite unable to go out unaccompanied.

Pamela was not, at the time, a committed Christian.
However, after being visited in hospital by Ann Barnett, our
Deaconess, she began to pray again. Ann had given her a
little booklet to encourage her, and had told her something of
God's power to heal her. This was the beginning of a new and
deeper relationship with God for Pamela, and she began to
pray for her healing. When Pamela came home, she also
began to be seen regularly by one of our pastoral visitors.
They became close friends, almost like sisters. Pamela had
heard much about life at St Mark's and longed to come along
one Sunday, but she felt a strange fear about coming which
kept her at home.

However, one Sunday she decided she could put it off no
longer, and she came along to the morning service. From
then on she determined to fight her fears of being alone and
doing things alone. In due course she was able to come to a
midweek service of prayer for healing. During the meditation, the 'Ring of Peace', she became acutely aware of

Christ's presence and of his deep peace. She went forward for prayers with laying on of hands, and left the service feeling really happy and contented. In the days that followed her confidence began to return, her depression lifted, and so did her fear of being alone. Her movements became lively and normal again – but her angina remained!

A few months later Pamela had another serious angina attack and many more were to follow. We all continued to pray that the angina would be healed, but it was not. One Sunday morning, Pamela collapsed after the service with another attack. I remember feeling a deep sense of frustration and anger that the illness still had such a grip on her. I immediately anointed her with oil, laid hands on her and – together with her close friend – we prayed for her healing. Instantly her breathing returned to normal, the pain disappeared and she felt that deep sense of peace once again. We believed that God had healed her, and she felt so fit and happy as she went home for dinner. For three months she was marvellous, but then she suffered another attack and found herself back in hospital.

Ever since then Pamela has been up and down with her health, and has been in and out of hospital. I have felt tremendous frustration that time and again she appears to have been healed after prayer, yet always the angina has returned. However, Pamela *has* received the healing of all her other complaints, and *has* retained her deep sense of peace and confidence in God. She is aware that her whole attitude to her illness has changed entirely, in that her fear has gone, she no longer feels so angry and she has confidence that she is in God's care. We do not know why the angina has not yet ceased, but we still pray constantly for Pamela's healing.

Being Positive

Failure of any kind is always hard to accept. In Christian healing ministry apparent failure can be heartbreaking. Yet we must always realise that if we have prayed in faith for someone, then God *will* have responded, even though we may not see healing in the manner we would wish for or expect. It does not therefore follow that, because a person has not apparently been healed as we have prayed that he would, we have failed. We need always to remember that God is in complete control of this ministry – not us; that it is Christ's power that brings healing – not ours; and that there will be occasions when, like the disciples faced with the epileptic boy, we will be unable to bring God's healing power.

There can be many reasons why people are not healed – some of which we will be looking at shortly – but the fact that some people are not healed must not deter us from continuing to pray in faith for healing. I have known deep hurt and sadness, frustration and even anger when people I love dearly have not apparently been healed. But I cannot and must not give up praying for their healing, and for the healing of others. There will always be those who need healing; we have been given the task and privilege of bringing God's healing, so we must not allow ourselves to be put off, or to fail to continue to bring the healing hands of God to those who are in need. Instead, we must thank God for all who *are* being healed, and gratefully move on, trusting in his longing to use us as channels of his healing love and power.

When little Susan died of cancer (see chapter 3), we felt that we had failed her. Many doubted the wisdom of our praying for her so openly, and building up the hopes of her family, only to see our prayers apparently frustrated when she died. It was the nearest we ever came to the point of turning back. But then we had to realise that God *had* heard our prayers and responded with love; he *had* cared for both Susan and her family throughout their ordeal; and finally he *had* healed her in what must have been the best way. It will always be hard to accept such a healing and I suppose it will always hurt, but if we have prayed in faith for God's healing, then he *has* responded, and we have not failed!

2. Why Some are not Healed

Twelve Reasons

No doubt there are many reasons why people are not healed, and we can never hope to know or understand them all. If we could, we would know the full wisdom of God! However, there *are* some reasons why people are not healed that we can perceive, and not only that, for having become aware of such barriers to healing, we can work and pray towards having them removed.

Eight of the twelve barriers I am going to mention are blockages within the person who is in need of healing, and four are in the ministry of those praying for the sick. If we are aware of such possible barriers to a person's being healed, we can do our best towards removing many of them before we begin to pray for healing.

i) Unwillingness to accept healing

It may seem strange that Jesus should have asked the cripple by the pool if he wanted to get well,[3] and yet that question must have needed asking. Over many years the cripple would have learned how to live with and use his infirmity to get by. Would he be able to cope with being healthy? That was what Jesus was asking him. There must be many today who have been unemployed for some considerable time, who faithfully visit the jobcentre each week, and yet who have become so used to unemployment that they might not now be able to cope with the possibility of having a job. This is the way we tend to be, and we get used to allowing our circumstances to dictate our way of life. The experience of taking three months' sabbatical leave to write this book has helped me to realise too just how much I allow my circumstances to dominate my parish life!

Most people who have been ill for a long time will have learned how to use their illness to their advantage. I am not trying to be unkind here, but it seems to be a natural human instinct to use our weaknesses to our advantage. For example, the partially-deaf person can hear what he wants to hear; the person who suffers from headaches can switch them on to escape doing things he doesn't want to do; and the person who is feeling a bit sorry for himself can use his illness to gain a little extra attention, sympathy or understanding – as and when he chooses! We can soon get used to using illness to our benefit without even realising it, and when we think hard about the possibility of managing without that prop, which we can use as we choose, we just might not really want to get well after all. Jesus knew when to check whether a person really wanted to be healed, or when to challenge whether he could cope with being whole again. We too must learn the need to be sure that a person really wants to get better. If he doesn't it will become a barrier to his healing.

ii) Resistance to God's Will

I know of people who, though they would very much like to get well again, are not prepared to let God have his say in their lives. Some back away instantly at the mere thought of being healed by God through prayer; others come forward – sometimes regularly – asking for prayers for healing, but wishing to dictate the terms, and not being prepared to let God have his way with them. This can be a solid barrier to healing which the sick person must deal with himself if he really wants to get better. The sort of person who resists in this way will usually place a high price on his independence, and might not be keen to become dependent upon Christ, even for healing.

In the last chapter I wrote about Paul, who was healed of colitis as he made a full commitment of his life to Christ. In the next section, I will be writing of Michelle who was not fully healed until she too came forward to make a personal commitment. Resistance to God's will shuts out his healing power, as we refuse him the freedom to work his will in our lives!

iii) Rejecting the Medicine

If I visit the doctor about my illness and he prescribes some medicine to clear up the trouble, which I refuse to take, then I can have no complaints if I fail to get better. When Naaman visited Elisha,[4] he totally rejected the method or 'medicine' which the prophet recommended. Had his servants not persuaded him to bathe seven times in the Jordan, he would not have been healed. Sometimes I become aware of certain steps a person needs to take before he can be healed, and I am able to share this (even though he may be well aware of it already!). Perhaps someone else needs to be forgiven, maybe some other sin needs putting right; it could be that a person's life needs 'cleaning up' or that a new relationship with God needs to be established. Whatever the reasons might be, if a person chooses to reject such medicine, then he should not be surprised when healing does not come!

iv) Sin

As we have already seen, a person's sinfulness can be the cause of his illness. Jesus warned the man he had healed by the pool to stop sinning, or else something worse might happen to him,[5] and we have seen that on other occasions Jesus realised that a person's sinfulness had brought on his sickness. It is therefore clear that sins must be dealt with before healing can come. This is why an act of penitence beforehand is encouraged, with the pronouncement of God's forgiveness.

v) Not Looking after Oneself

A person who does not look after his health is always liable to become ill. In order to get well again he may need to pay more attention to his cleanliness, his diet, his habits or whatever else is at the root of his complaint. People who don't look after their teeth must expect toothache before too long; those who allow themselves to become overweight must eventually expect trouble with legs or heart; heavy smokers are more open to lung cancer and heavy drinkers to stomach and liver complaints; people who overwork leave their bodies open to all kinds of illness, and so the list goes on. It's little use asking God, the doctor or anyone else to help us if we are not prepared to help ourselves by leading a balanced and sensible life.

vi) Bad Relationships

Enough has already been mentioned about the ways in which bad relationships can cause various kinds of mental and physical illness. If a person is not prepared to put right wrong relationships, then the cause remains and the healing cannot be effected.

vii) Lack of Keenness

If we want to be healed, it is good to show God that we mean business about it. If we come forward with our request in a casual sort of way to 'see if anything happens', then we may be disappointed. I know of one or two people who have asked for healing in this way and have not been made well, but who have later asked for healing in a more careful and determined way, and have then been healed.

June had been feeling tired and jaded for about three weeks. She was suffering from constant headaches and neck pains and had asked for healing in the course of her daily prayers, but matters had not improved. She felt that more urgency in her prayers was called for. She took a tablet (!), prayed for healing with real determination and received the healing she asked for.

viii) Lack of Personal Faith

Sometimes Jesus would look for signs of faith in a sick person, and it is clear that personal faith can sometimes be necessary for healing to take place. Lack of faith can be a barrier to healing. Many do not even have the faith that God wants to heal them, and choose to bear their sickness with patient endurance; others do not believe that Christ can heal today, or cannot accept that his power and love can conquer *their* illness. Faith in Christ's longing, ability and willingness to heal is, as we have seen, a great step towards actually receiving healing.

ix) Lack of Prayer Faith

When the disciples could not heal the epileptic boy, Jesus blamed their lack of faith.[1] Sometimes when we pray for the healing of the sick, it may be our lack of faith which is the barrier to their being healed. Perhaps we feel that the illness is too serious or too far advanced, or maybe that the person has been ill for too long, for us to really believe that God can or will heal the sick person. If those who pray for healing have not faith in God's willingness and ability to heal, then healing may not come. Yet if there is a little faith within a church, then as we see more and more healings, our faith in God will grow, and the barrier of lack of faith will be lifted.

x) Lack of Prayer Keenness

Those who pray for the healing of others need also to show God that we mean business about it. A casual attitude to prayer for healing which lacks love, determination and expectation can become a barrier to healing. I believe that we went through a barren year in our prayers for healing because we had lost that sense of keenness in our prayers. Days of Prayer, fasting and perseverance may be needed to lift such barriers.

xi) Wrong Diagnosis

If a doctor diagnoses wrongly the nature of an illness, then the wrong kind of medicine or treatment will fail to cure the problem, and could even make matters worse. Similarly, if we diagnose wrongly the nature of a person's illness, we too are liable to respond in the wrong manner, and could make matters worse. If we pray for physical healing when the need is for prayer for inner healing, if we pray for inner healing when the need is for deliverance, if we pray for deliverance when there is a physical or mental problem – then our prayers may be futile because we have failed to discern the true nature of the trouble.

xii) Tackling only the Symptoms

As we have already seen, most physical illnesses seem to have an emotional cause of some kind. Very often the healing can only be effected when we have prayerfully reached the root-cause of the sickness – whether it is to do with memories, relationships or feelings. Sometimes it is just not sufficient to pray for the healing of the physical problem, but we need to find the source and focus or prayers there.

Ever since she stopped smoking four years previously, Sylvia had suffered from regular migraines, from which tablets brought little relief. She was present at one of our healing services and decided on impulse to come forward for the healing of these migraines. There was no resultant improvement whatsoever. Some time later she mentioned this, and we sat down together to try to seek prayerfully the causes of the trouble. When we were able to see the number of stresses she was under – domestic, in relationships, in voluntary work, in her part-time job and studies – it no longer seemed surprising that she suffered from migraines. Sylvia began to make some changes in her pattern of life, we prayed about these root-causes and then she came forward at an evening Communion service for prayer for healing with laying on of hands. She has not been troubled with migraines since.

3. Patience and Perseverance

We have considered some of the barriers or blockages to healing that occur, and that we may be able to remove. Yet there are other reasons why people may not be healed, or why healing may be progressive or delayed, and we must look at these too.

I believe that sometimes God is prepared to allow (not cause!) sickness, in order to achieve some higher purpose. I have known much good to come out of sickness in other ways, or through delayed healings. People have come to faith, have gained a deeper appreciation of health, have had the course of their lives changed, have averted disasters – all through sickness. We cannot see the whole of life as God can, and whilst he will never cause sickness, it does seem that sometimes by allowing it he can achieve his higher purposes for us. We must therefore be patient in prayer for healing, accepting that he is responding to our prayers, and that he really will do what is best for us – always!

Progressive Healings

It has been my experience that a great number of healings through prayer are progressive. I have already offered many examples of such healings. It is important that we realise this, for too many people want and expect instant action in our age of instant everything. When Jesus healed the blind man at Bethsaida,[6] the healing was progressive, and today in Christian healing ministry so often the healing comes about progressively, sometimes even over years. No doubt it is best that so many healings are progressive, for I wonder how many of us could actually cope with instant healing! When healing does seem to be coming about progressively, and maybe quite slowly, it is important that we thank God for each step of improvement, however small it may be, and in this way our faith will grow as the healing grows too.

Vera's breakdown was sudden and unexpected. As a committed member of St Mark's she was much involved in many aspects of our ministry, and was keen to grow and develop in her Christian faith. Over a long period, she had had a number of extremely hurtful experiences, some of which centred around those she loved and prayed for who had apparently not been healed. With the build-up of these hurts, the unanswered questions and various other things she felt unable to cope with, Vera suffered a complete emotional and spiritual breakdown.

We ministered to her and prayed for her healing, but soon began to feel out of our depth, and in due course she was admitted to a psychiatric hospital for treatment. During the several weeks she was in hospital, we prayed for her healing, supporting her family as we could by offering transport to the hospital, and various members visited her. Improvement seemed to be very slow, but we continued to pray with patience and perseverance.

Vera remembers nothing of her time in hospital until Easter Day, when she went to the hospital chapel. Then everything slowly began to fall into place for her, as she grew steadily better and better. After another fortnight she was discharged, and now weeks later, she has completely recovered. Vera's healing was gradual; it was effected through medical treatment (by injections), counselling in hospital, and the patient and persevering prayer of her own family, and her family at St Mark's.

Delayed Healings

As we have also seen, healing may be delayed for many reasons – usually beyond our knowledge. Barriers may need to be lifted, faith may need time to grow, God may have some higher purpose, or perhaps we may just need to learn patience and perseverance. I used to be surprised at the number of healings that would not become evident for quite a time. Nowadays I tell people in advance that delay is quite likely!

Michelle was twenty-one when she had rheumatic fever. This left her with a twisted foot and a bad limp which caused difficulty with any kind of climbing. She would usually crawl up stairs, and it was very painful for her to walk up hills. She was a timid and nervous person – probably because of this – and she eventually began to feel that she was gradually losing the use of her legs through stiffness.

One Ash Wednesday she came forward for prayers for healing with laying on of hands at the evening service. She asked God to heal her. Afterwards she felt disappointed that nothing seemed to have changed, and she began to feel guilty about this. Yet a healing had taken place, for about a fortnight later Michelle began to realise that she felt much more relaxed than usual, and that she was not needing her indigestion tablets any more. Previously she had suffered from nervous indigestion; she had not asked for healing of *that*, but that was what had been healed!

Still Michelle wanted to have her legs healed, and continued to pray for their healing. About six months later she came to another service of prayer for healing. When she came forward this time, she asked nothing of God. Instead she made a new commitment of her life, and gave over all her worries to him. Again she was disappointed and upset, as she left the church limping just as she had come. But three days later her disappointment vanished.

She awoke early, jumped out of bed and actually ran down the stairs. She was astonished when she realised what she had done. Michelle kept the news to herself until the following day, by which time she found that she could walk quite normally. She was excited to hear the clicking of her heels as she walked, instead of her former shuffling. Still Michelle felt reluctant to share her excitement, in case it was just a short remission. When at last she realised her healing was real, she chose to show her husband, rather than to tell him, but felt frustrated that at first he didn't seem to notice. She went upstairs and began stamping around in the bedroom, but even then he paid little attention. Finally she decided to run up and down the stairs a few times, then he would have to notice – and he did!

Since then, not only has Michelle lost her limp completely, but also her character has been transformed. Gone is the timid and nervous little figure, replaced by a quietly confident lady who lives each day to serve God by serving others. She feels a new person, her nerves no longer trouble her and she loves to tell the tale of her healing to any who wish to hear it. Family and friends have all noticed the incredible change, and her ministry to others is now quite extensive.

Michelle's healing was delayed until she was able to make a full commitment of her life to Christ. When that healing came, it was far more than she had asked for or dreamed she might receive. She was made completely whole, she discovered a new life that was really worth living and today she is one of our church elders.

Coping with Suffering

Time and again the world has asked why a righteous God does not put an end to the suffering caused by sickness. There have been many attempts to give reasons for human suffering. Many thought-provoking theories and propositions have been put forward. Whilst these can be helpful in understanding the nature and cost of human freedom, I do not propose to discuss them further as they are rarely of much help or encouragement to those who are actually suffering through illness.

What I do want to do is to make some important affirmations concerning this kind of suffering:

1. Although this is clearly a part of the world we live in, it is not God's will that we should suffer. There is no way that a loving heavenly Father could derive pleasure or satisfaction of any kind from seeing his children suffer. If ever we begin to accept suffering as being the will of God, then we reduce our image of God to that of a cruel tyrant, and our faith becomes fear.

2. We can be sure that God really understands what suffering is all about, for in the death of his Son he shared the worst kind of suffering that the world has to offer. He is not a distant deity who neither knows nor cares about our sufferings. He is a loving Father who feels and shares in all our deepest pains and hurts.

3. God not only understands and shares in our suffering, but he has also given us all the resources we need to cope with it. Even though we may suffer greatly through illness or disability or hurt, God has promised his children all the strength that we will need to be able to cope. We will never be tried beyond our resources – God will not allow it!

4. God enables us to use our suffering for good. If we allow such suffering to dominate our lives, then we become morbid and sorry for ourselves, and faith fails. If we allow God to dominate our sickness or suffering, by focussing on

his love and power, then it will be used to his purposes. Many have come to faith through such a witness, and continue to thank God for his blessings!

5. Finally, God has given mankind the most wonderful gift of love, love which we can use in caring for those who are ill or suffering and easing their discomfort. God may not have lifted all suffering out of the world, but he has given us everything we need to cope with it, conquer it and use it to his good purposes.

Rosemary, a committed member of our congregation, developed breast cancer. She delayed going to see her doctor about it and, despite radio-therapy treatment, the family was eventually informed that the illness would be terminal. We continued to pray with perseverance for her healing, members of the congregation would call to see her each day, and we did our best to make her life more fulfilling by keeping her in touch with all that was going on and taking her mind off the illness and on to God. At first, Rosemary would talk a great deal about her illness and little else. She became depressed and upset and felt that she was losing her faith. But members of the church showed great love and sensitivity in ever so gently turning her around to focus on God. Her family were marvellous in their care for her, and she became a much more patient patient. No longer would she speak of her illness, but through it she became a fine witness to God. Sadly, she always resisted talking of her possible death, but then she was ready anyway. She died peacefully some months ago.

Ministry to Those who are not yet Healed

Whilst it is a part of our ministry to bring Christ's healing to the sick, it is also a part of our ministry to care for those who do not get well. This care must involve many practical expressions of love, and can be very costly in patience, time and effort.

Many fear to step into Christian healing ministry because

they are most concerned about the possible consequences for those who may not be healed; could we be building up false hopes? might they feel bitter? will they lose faith? and so on. Whilst these are genuine concerns, it has not been my experience that this is what usually happens. Everyone seems to receive something, and if together we can see what this is, then faith is strengthened and not diminished. Some seem to find new hope and others a new sense of purpose; many experience a deep sense of God's peace; others are challenged to look carefully at their whole lives. God cares deeply for all who are not yet healed, and he needs us to reveal that love to them.

One of our major tasks is to build up the hopes of the sick person. We can make no wild promises, for only God can know how healing and wholeness will come, but what we can do is to offer the assurance of God's continuing love and care to those who are not yet healed. He longs to heal everyone and eventually he will do so, even if it is by the 'final healing'.

The 'Final Healing'

Part of our ministry and care should involve preparing people for the 'final healing' that comes at death – or 'new life' as I much prefer to call it. I find it so sad that in our culture we so rarely speak of death or face up to it, and that this inevitably leads to a widespread fear of death and dying. There is no fear in death for the Christian, and this we must share with all around us, for it will be for us the most wondrous and joyful experience we will ever know.

Eventually we must all grow old and die – we have to face up to this fact. When we pray for the healing of someone very old or seriously ill, we must be aware that healing may come through death. Death is God's final way of healing us. Many have asked me how they should pray for someone who is likely to die. I encourage all to continue to pray for healing, bearing in mind that it may have to come through death. In this way, we can leave the nature of healing safely in the hands of God, which is always the sensible approach anyway! I believe this is a positive approach which can be of great hope and encouragement to all.

One evening when I was visiting a patient in Broadgreen Hospital, I was approached by a lady who seemed very upset. She explained the reason for her distress. She was waiting outside the ward where her father, who had suffered a major heart attack, lay dying, whilst a few wards away her mother too was near to death through pneumonia and kidney failure following an accident in which she had broken her leg. She had just sat down in the corridor and prayed that a clergyman would come along who could give them both the 'last rites'. I went with her to see each of them. I laid hands on them both and together we prayed that God would heal them, allowing that such healing might well be in the 'new life'. Some time later she wrote to me explaining that her father had died peacefully shortly after I had left. Her mother, however, had made a remarkable recovery and was soon able to walk again with the aid of a zimmer. At the time she was ninety years old! I believe that both parents were healed. It can never be inappropriate, nor too late, to pray for healing!

When ministering to those who are facing death, I believe that honesty is the best policy, though sadly I find that this is often difficult. Sometimes the family decides that a person should not know the nature of his illness, or its likely outcome. Sometimes the person himself will firmly avoid any talk of death. We should try gently and sensitively to encourage all to be honest and speak of the possibility of death, though in the end we must respect the wishes of the person or his family in this matter, and not force the truth upon them. When a person has come to terms with the possibility of death in the near future, often the stress will cease, peace comes and he is able to slip naturally, gently and confidently into his new life.

Just as the pain of suffering can be conquered by trust in God's love, so too can the fear of death. We must continue to pray for healing, but we can confidently leave the matter of whether that healing is to be in this life or the next in the hands of God.

Martin was once a strong and healthy police officer, but then he began to suffer from one of the most cruel illnesses I have ever known. It is called Huntington's Chorea and is a hereditary disease of the nervous system which eventually, over a long period, leads to the loss of the use of every muscle. Martin had had the illness for eight years and Frances, his wife, was beginning to find it difficult to cope as he grew worse. Then she met Michelle, one of our elders, who soon began to call regularly and to do anything she could to help Frances with looking after her husband. Soon they discovered that Don, Michelle's husband, was an old friend of Martin's, and he too began to call regularly to chat over old times with Martin, a task that needed patience and perseverance for Martin's speech was now very difficult to understand, and much of the conversation had to be one-way traffic. Although Martin had great difficulty with speech, he could still understand everything clearly, and he experienced and expressed deep frustration at his inability to make himself clearly understood.

We prayed for Martin's healing with laying on of hands and whilst his physical condition didn't improve, his ability to cope with it certainly did. He became less frustrated, not so violent and unpredictable, much quieter and more at peace. By now Frances had become a committed Christian, and she too felt much at peace with the situation, knowing that God was taking care of everything. She was also able to benefit greatly from the support of Michelle, Don and other members of St Mark's.

Don and Michelle offered to take Frances and Martin with them on a caravan holiday, and the offer was gladly accepted. For the first week they were all able to enjoy a great time together, but then it all appeared to become too much for Martin; he became very restless and at times violent and angry. They decided to return home, but the drive became a nightmare as Martin continually thrashed about and struggled to get out of the moving car. They prayed that they would reach home safely, for Martin's behaviour was becoming a danger to them all and making driving extremely hazardous for Don. They completed the journey safely, but Martin was admitted immediately to a psychiatric hospital. He refused to settle, and pleaded with Frances to take him home again. This caused her heartbreak, for she knew she couldn't look after him at home any longer. She prayed for his peace of mind, and he settled down.

For a year, Martin's condition remained much the same, and Frances was able to enjoy many pleasant times with him, walking together around the hospital grounds and sometimes sitting in the sunshine. Others visited him too, including Dave Florence, our Church Army Captain, and it was clear that he appreciated these visits and the opportunities to spend a little time together in prayer. By now we had all left the manner of his healing in the Lord's hands.

Then Martin began to weaken and his condition started to deteriorate. Frances asked Michelle and Don to pray with her that God would now 'find a place for him in his heaven'. Three days later he died peacefully, and they were able to thank God for his goodness. Martin had been healed at last!

Notes

1. Matt. 17:14-21
2. Mark 9:28-29
3. John 5:6
4. 2 Kgs. 5:1-14
5. John 5:14
6. Mark 8:22-26

Chapter 11

A SHARED MINISTRY OF HEALING

In the chapters that follow, I want to look briefly at some of the practicalities of Christian healing ministry – how we can go about it. Within the scope of this book it is not possible or necessary to go fully into the background or reasoning behind these directions. Many other writers have done this thoroughly already, as I will indicate.

What I want to offer are suggestions for guidelines in this ministry, with simple explanations of the whys and wherefores. I hope you will therefore understand the need for brevity, and find these suggestions helpful in support of your ministry of prayer for healing.

1. The Need for Shared Ministry

The Role of the Priest/Minister/Pastor

Whilst in some Churches and traditions much of Christian ministry is seen as being the individual responsibility of the priest or minister, in others more emphasis is laid on the corporate or shared ministry of the Church. I believe that there is not only room, but also need, for both approaches together. There are times when it is a priestly type of ministry that seems to be called for, a one-to-one, confidential response, which may also be more formal and involving sacraments. There are other occasions when the need is for a shared ministry, with strong communal prayer, faith and caring.

Jesus conducted a dynamic personal ministry to the many who came to him. But then he also shared that ministry, very closely with his chosen twelve, and more widely with the commissioning of the seventy. When he healed, sometimes he acted alone, sometimes with just a few of the twelve and often with a very wide circle of others involved.

Today the priest, minister or pastor is still called upon to exercise a very personal ministry as and when this seems appropriate. But I believe that he is also being called upon more and more to share most areas of ministry with others, to spend a great deal of his time and energy in enabling others to play a full and leading part in the ongoing ministry of the Church. The ministry of prayer for healing needs to be both personal and shared.

When Jack arrived at the vicarage it was clearly a personal ministry that was needed. He was nervous, anxious and suffering from extreme depression, and he seemed to be reaching the end of his tether. He sat down and explained how his life seemed to be falling apart around him, all because he happened to be in the wrong place at the wrong time. He had gone out one evening in order to help someone else in need, as a result of which he had finished up by being arrested and accused of a serious crime. As a result of this he was suspended from his job and was awaiting trial.

He just couldn't believe it was all really happening. He felt absolutely shattered and dismayed, and it was only the love and support of his family that he felt was keeping him going at all. In his own mind he had himself convicted and put behind bars. It was like living through a nightmare; he felt awful, and he didn't know what to do.

Jack was not a member of St Mark's; he was a casual sort of Christian who occasionally attended another church. Now he felt angry with God that he had been badly let down, and he needed to talk this out with a minister. A friend had suggested he came to see me. Jack wanted to talk about why God had apparently deserted him in this way. He had always had faith in God, though he was aware that it was probably lacking in many ways, but now he felt that faith was fading fast and he wanted clear assurance of God's continuing care for him.

Together we looked over Jack's situation, positively and

realistically. Although it was clearly an awful situation for anyone to find himself in, there were many positive features, and it seemed most unlikely that he would ever be convicted. Yet still he felt so anxious, and more deeply depressed than he had ever known. He was filled with self-pity and felt that God had abandoned him.

Jack and I went over together to the church. There we knelt down and carefully asked God to take over and manage every aspect of this terrible situation. Then Jack came forward and knelt at the Communion rail. I gently laid hands on his head and prayed that God would lift his depression, remove all the anxiety and fill Jack with the knowledge of his love. That prayer was answered instantly. Jack was immediately overtaken by a deep sense of peacefulness and calm, he could smile again, and he left the church a very different person from the one who came.

His ordeal dragged on for eighteen months, with the hearing being postponed time and again. Throughout this time his peacefulness about the situation lasted and grew, in spite of these setbacks, and moments of doubt and depression were brief. Meanwhile he experienced many encouraging signs of God's love and care for him as he was led gently through this very traumatic period. Jack's situation called for a personal ministry of God's healing. Recently he was cleared of all charges, and he is now back at work.

David's situation called for corporate ministry. He was suffering from a sclerosis of the retina in his left eye which caused a limit in the angle of his vision. This had been discovered by his optician, who referred him to his doctor, and he in turn referred David to the Eye Hospital where he was offered an appointment six months later. As an elder, David shared this with the rest of the group, and together we prayed that his eye might be healed. When David kept his appointment at the hospital a thorough examination revealed no trace of the problem.

I would recommend a really helpful section on 'Personal Ministry' in Morris Maddock's book *The Christian Healing Ministry* (see appendix 2).

'Body Ministry'

No priest or pastor can ever cope with all his ministerial responsibilities on his own – he needs the rest of the 'body', just as they need him. He needs their prayers and many kinds of practical support. More even than this, he needs their love and cares, and he will often need their guidance too. This applies to the ministry of prayer for healing as much as anything else.

I believe that the best way to effect this kind of shared ministry is to follow Christ's pattern by choosing a small group (up to twelve) to take on special responsibilities in ministry. It is such a group that can best offer the close and committed support that a priest or pastor needs, and also spearhead the whole ministry of the church. This group might be called the church leaders, or church elders, depending upon the exact nature of its role. The group is not a rival to the Church Council or similar body, but rather a group that is called to serve the church by carefully guiding and participating in its ministries of teaching, healing, caring and evangelising.

The group needs to be a 'body of prayer', committed to seeking God's guidance for the church by prayer and study, and communicating this to the whole congregation with active care and leadership. The group needs to develop a unity of trust and openness to one another, a depth of fellowship that will enable the group to stand strong in the times of trial and testing that will undoubtedly come. The members of the group will be much involved in prayers for healing with laying on of hands, as part of the church's normal ministry, and in making decisions about the course and nature of that ministry. That group should become an expression of corporate leadership for the local church, an inspiration to the members and a body of real support to the priest or pastor, and to one another.

But then, let us not forget that the ministry of prayer and care for the sick is not just the responsibility of this group; it is the ministry of the whole church – every single member.

2. Towards a Shared Ministry

Choosing and Preparing

Who are we to choose as elders or leaders? This is a matter that needs to be considered prayerfully over a long period of time. We need to pray for wisdom and guidance, the priest(s) or pastor(s) need to consider names and then pray again, looking for signs of confirmation. Eventually those thought to be called to this ministry need to be approached and asked to consider whether they feel called to serve in this way and to pray for guidance in this.

We can get some guidance for the sort of people we are looking for from the Letter to Titus.[1] We are not just seeking the professional type of person; Jesus chose ordinary men who were humble, honest and loyal. I believe that women should also be involved, for it has been my experience that the participation of women makes for a much more balanced form of leadership and ministry. The people we are looking for need to be people of faith and love who lead a holy life of prayer and commitment and who are well respected by all. The Letter to Titus suggests further qualities. The demands and responsibilities of this ministry need to be made clear beforehand, and are best laid down in writing and possibly signed by each person too, as an act of commitment.

Once the membership of the group has been agreed upon, it is important that the members begin to meet together to draw closer to one another and to prepare for their new ministry. Much discussion will be needed to determine the precise role of the group and the responsibilities each member is to have. This is an exciting and forward-looking time, and must be shared with the rest of the congregation to avoid suggestions of an 'in-group' or cliquiness.

Training and Commissioning

Jesus' training of his disciples was very much on the job training. They worked alongside him and he taught them in relation to the situations and problems they faced in their everyday ministry. Some may prefer to use structured training courses before commissioning, but I have always preferred this method of study and training which is closely related to where the group is heading. We must remember too that training and learning together never ends, and we should watch for opportunities locally to train and learn with and from other Christians.

There needs to be a formal commissioning of the new leaders or elders in a main service before the congregation. The nature of the group and the roles of its members need to be explained with care on this occasion, and repeated as often as possible, with great emphasis on the members' being called to serve the congregation, and not to boss them around! The group is called to be a prayer group rather than a power group, and it is vital that this is seen to be so. The commissioning should take place with the laying on of hands by the priest or pastor or perhaps a bishop or other leader.

When new members are to be added to the group, the approach needs to be in a similar manner, with the consensus of the whole group if possible. Some time ago I suggested to our church leaders that Audrey might join our group. Several leaders were unsure about this suggestion, and even after much prayer for guidance we were still divided in opinion. I had felt very strongly guided in this matter, so I suggested that we ask God for a clear sign. Audrey was deaf in her left ear, and had been so since childhood. We asked that God would enable her to hear again in that ear, if he was calling her to be a church leader.

At the next healing service Audrey came forward for prayer to ask for the ending of a recent bout of nightmares. Others were praying for the healing of deafness in her ear. A little while afterwards, Audrey's nightmares ceased, and then her left ear stopped discharging as it had always done previously. She also suffered from a stiffness in her neck, and that too began to ease. Then before long her hearing began to return. She now has permanent – though partial – hearing in her left ear, and at moments when she feels particularly close to God that hearing becomes complete. Audrey was invited to become one of the church leaders, and in due course she accepted and was commissioned.

It was as well that we had had this confirmation of the sign, for Audrey found it difficult to settle naturally into the group, and her presence began to hinder the openness that was previously present. Had it not been for the clear confirmation of that sign, we should have certainly doubted the wisdom of inviting her to join the group. As things turned out, Audrey was to learn a great deal about herself in being with us (at times it must have been difficult and hurtful to accept some of the things that were said, even though they were spoken in love and openness) but eventually we were all to benefit by her presence, and the group is now much stronger for this.

I have recorded this experience because I feel it reveals many pitfalls that may occur in the life of other leader or elder groups travelling along similar roads.

For further reading on shared ministry, I would recommend David Watson's chapters on 'Ministry and Leadership' in his book *I Believe in the Church* (see appendix 2).

3. Ministering Together

Praying for Healing with Laying on of Hands

A considerable number of Jesus' healing miracles were by touch or by the laying on of hands: 'he placed his hands on every one of them and healed them all' (Luke 4:40 GNB).[2] The laying on of hands had long been used for conferring God's blessing, his commissioning and for other forms of dedication in Old Testament times. Jesus used the laying on of hands for blessing and healing, and in the New Testament Church this was continued with further use of the practice for commissioning and dedication, and also for receiving the fullness of the Holy Spirit.

Here we are concerned mainly with the use of the laying on

of hands for healing, when a priest, pastor or group of elders gently lays hands on a person's head and prays for his healing.

There are three main reasons for following this practice. In the first place it was what Christ himself often did and also commanded his disciples to do.[3] Secondly, it became the practice of the early Church, and was seen to be effective in enabling God's healing power to flow through the ministers or elders to bring healing to the sick. There is also a third (human) benefit in this practice in that love and care are always communicated far better by touch than by words. There is something deeply moving about receiving laying on of hands.

It is vital that the laying on of hands is always accompanied with prayer – for healing or whatever else the practice is used for. I feel it is best that the practice is normally carried out by those commissioned to do so, unless there is good reason for involving others. This can avoid superstitions and other misunderstandings, or the misuse or belittling of this ministry. The laying on of hands can take place in a home or hospital, in a group meeting or church service, in a one-to-one pastoral situation or in an emergency.

We must always remember that it is Christ himself who heals, and not those involved in this ministry. As I have said, at St Mark's we know of no one who has a gift of healing, although we have found that sometimes members of the congregation have attempted to 'pin' a gift on to one or other of the elders or ministers. Whilst there may be those who have gifts of healing,[4] the source of that power is God himself.

In these ways, I believe that the practice of prayer for healing with laying on of hands should always be a part of the natural ministry of the church, though we must be careful that it never becomes casual or loses its specialness.

It was a Sunday, and my wife had been troubled by a severe headache all day. In the evening it was the elders' meeting in the vicarage, but she had to leave the meeting to go and lie down because it was causing her such distress. It was the worst headache she had had ever known. During our prayer time we naturally prayed for her, and afterwards I went upstairs to see how she was. She felt dreadful. So there and then I gently laid hands on her head and prayed that God would lift the headache. It disappeared instantly – much to her astonishment – and she was able to drift gently off to sleep.

For further reading on the practice of laying on of hands, I would recommend John Richards' pamphlet *Laying on of Hands*, and Morris Maddocks' section on the subject in his book *The Christian Healing Ministry* (see appendix 2).

The Anointing of the Sick

The practice of anointing the sick with olive oil was used by the twelve when Jesus first sent them out,[5] and in the early Church,[6] that they might be healed. Later it came to be used in preparing a person for death ('Last Rites'), in the consecration of kings and priests (as in the Old Testament) and with Baptism and Confirmation.

The anointing with oil is a sacramental act which proclaims our unity with Christ. It is through the anointing that our oneness with him is symbolised and restored, and it usually takes place in the context of prayer with laying on of hands. It should normally be administered by the priest or pastor, with the support of the church leaders or elders and in similar settings and situations to other prayer for healing with laying on of hands.

A key question seems to be when to anoint the sick and when to simply pray with laying on of hands. There are many views on this matter, but I feel that anointing should be the exception rather than the norm. I have tended to anoint those who have been suffering from either serious or persistent illness, and I have done so in many different situations.

It often seems best to set the anointing in the context of an informal little service involving a reading from Scripture and possibly meditation, prayers – including prayers of confession, absolution and thanksgiving – and the singing of an appropriate hymn or song. For the anointing ordinary olive oil is used (readily obtainable from the chemist) which, if not previously consecrated by bishop or minister, can be consecrated just before the anointing. The anointing is usually administered by the priest or pastor putting olive oil on his thumb and then making the sign of the cross with it on the forehead of the sick person.

This practice seems to be being revived amongst Christians of all traditions, and in the Anglican Church the service of the blessing of oils by the bishop occurs in cathedrals all over the country on Maundy Thursday. The oil is then taken out to the parishes for use by the local church amongst its members who are ill.

For further reading on the practice of anointing, I would recommend John Richards' pamphlet *Anointing*, and Morris Maddocks' section on the subject in his book *The Christian Healing Ministry* (see appendix 2).

Notes

1. see Titus 1:5-9
2. see also Luke 13:13
3. Mark 16:18
4. see I Cor. 12:28
5. Mark 6:13
6. Jas. 5:14

Chapter 12

SERVICES OF PRAYER FOR HEALING

1. The Time and the Place

Special Healing Services

Christian healing ministry is part of the whole ministry of the Church and should therefore never be regarded as a separate or fringe activity. It needs to be at the heart of a church's normal life, and for this reason many would avoid special healing services, preferring instead to retain prayers for healing within the context of the main Sunday services. Whilst I would not argue with this view, I do maintain that there is also a place for special services of prayer for healing.

Special healing services offer a considerable number of additional opportunities which I believe can be very important. I use the word *special* because they always offer the chance to focus on the specialness of this part of our ministry. Such a service provides opportunity for special concern with teaching and guidance in this matter, and for creating a really positive setting in which this ministry can take place. More time can be spent in preparing for the service with the undivided attention of the whole congregation, and this leads to a build-up in confidence and expectation that God is going to heal. This type of service also becomes open to a wider circle of people from the local community or other churches and many Christians find it easier to come forward in such a setting, rather than on their own at a Sunday service.

Such services are particularly helpful and appropriate in the early days, when the ministry of prayer for healing with laying on of hands is first being introduced to the congregation. It enables this necessary focus and does not disturb the Sunday worship for those who feel it might. For this reason it is best that they should take place on a weekday – possibly midweek – with maximum publicity amongst the congregation and a quieter advertising in the wider community. I believe that we need to make the local community aware of this ministry as a part of the challenge of Christ, but it should never be publicised in a glamorous way as a means of drawing people into church.

It is difficult to decide how often such services should be held. We have found that three or four times a year seems to be about right, so long as there are other provisions within the ongoing life of the church. We have found it helpful to use some of the feast days and saints' days of the Church's calendar on which to hold the services. Beforehand we hold a short Communion service for those who wish to prepare by receiving Communion.

I now offer some suggestions for the format of a special service of prayer for healing. Clearly the exact nature of the service will depend very much on the customs and tradition of the local church, but I list below some of the elements which we have found to be especially appropriate and helpful.

Welcome and Introduction
The service needs to begin with some words from the 'president' by way of explanation of the nature of the service, and to enable the congregation to feel relaxed and comfortable. 'The Peace' might also be shared.

Praise
At the beginning of the service we need to focus on God's power, love and care as brought to us in Christ. All healing

comes through him. Suitable well-known hymns and prayers of praise can help to create a sense of dependent expectation.

The Word
There are many aspects of Christ's healing ministry upon which we can focus, as you must now be aware. Reading(s) from Scripture, appropriate to the chosen theme, can be expounded in the address, which should offer both gentle challenge and loving encouragement.

The Prayers
Prayers need to be in accordance with the custom of the local church – formal, extempore or shared. They should include a time of silent prayer (for the unloading of worries or burdens), and opportunity for confession and absolution.

Meditation
I have found that a conducted meditation on one of Jesus' healing miracles is a most helpful prelude to prayer for healing. After reading from Scripture, the leader might recreate the scene in the minds of the congregation, enabling all to focus on the healing power of Christ. Alternatively the 'Ring of Peace' might be used (see chapter 2, note 1).

The Invitation
The invitation to come forward for prayer should be explicit and encouraging, without being pushing. People need to know when to come forward, how to come forward and what to do when they get there. It is also vital to make it clear that the invitation is open to everyone (including children), and that reasons for coming forward may include any kind of healing, great or small; healing on behalf of someone else; as an act of thanksgiving for a healing; to make a personal commitment; as an act of prayer-commitment for a particular concern; or even to ask to be filled with the power of God's Holy Spirit. People should be left free either to come forward and kneel in silence, or to mention why they have come forward if they wish.

The Prayers for Healing

As people come forward, quiet background music can be helpful. Afterwards, a gentle hymn or song of thanksgiving is probably the most sensitive way of continuing the service.

The Close of the Service

This is as important a part of the service as any, for it determines where we 'leave people' as they leave the building. There needs to be an element of thanksgiving for God's coming to us to heal, a sense of commissioning, for we are healed to serve and witness and live a whole life (the closing collect of the morning prayer service of the Anglican Alternative Service Book is most appropriate) and a word of blessing emphasising God's continuing care for us. A final hymn that expresses joyfully one or more of these elements will send everyone out on a positive and encouraging note.

One or two other points are worth remembering. If you choose to bring in a guest speaker, be sure that his style of ministry is similar to that which the local church is developing. If he shares in the prayer for healing with laying on of hands, make sure that it is amongst the local ministers, ordained and lay, and not on his own. The laying on of hands always seems to take considerably longer than anticipated (more people usually come forward than we expect), and this should be taken account of in the planning of the service. An overall service of about an hour and a quarter seems to be about right. The flow of the service should not be interrupted by notices. If these have to be made, they are best at the beginning. Some clergy publicly offer opportunities for counselling afterwards, but many people find this off-putting. I would suggest instead the provision of somewhere for people to stay behind for a cup of tea afterwards, where more informal counselling can take place as necessary.

Prayers for Healing at Sunday Services

It should be our aim, in due course, to introduce the ministry of prayers for healing with laying on of hands into the main

Sunday worship of the church. How and when this might be
will again depend much on the customs and tradition of the
local church. We have found a Sunday evening Communion
service to be most appropriate.

The Communion service will always be an excellent setting, for Communion is all about healing and wholeness.
Some suggest the most appropriate point in the service is
during the intercessions, others prefer after 'The Peace', and
many pray for a person immediately after he or she has
received Communion. Our practice is to ask those who seek
prayer for healing (by arrangement beforehand) to come
forward for Communion after everyone else, and then to
remain at the Communion rail at the end, when the ministers
and elders who have been administering Communion will
pray for the person with laying on of hands. Some churches
will find other forms of morning or evening service to be
equally suitable.

Prayers for Healing on Other Occasions

There will be other settings in the church's life where this
ministry will seem to be appropriate. Midweek fellowship
groups or house groups may offer the best environment for a
quieter, less formal time of prayer for the healing of one of the
members of the group.

In such cases this needs to be set in the context of a
mini-service involving much more briefly the various aspects
of a special healing service. I have found that the practice of
anointing seems to be quite natural in such a setting.

At one of our midweek fellowship meetings, Edna had
asked that we anoint her and pray for her healing from
Parkinson's disease. When Michael heard about this, he
asked us to anoint him too as he had been suffering from
persistent headaches. Both were regular members of the
group, so at one of our meetings we held a little service during
which we prayed for them both and anointed them with
laying on of hands. Both had carefully prepared themselves
for this ministry. For Edna, there were no apparent signs of

improvement at all at the time. For Michael, the headaches continued for a week or so and then lifted.

Prayer for healing with laying on of hands is also important as a part of the everyday personal ministry of ministers such as clergy and elders. It is often a natural climax to a counselling session, a sick visit or in an emergency. I have also felt it appropriate with the Baptism of a sick child. Christopher was just six weeks old and facing a dangerous operation in hospital from which his chances of survival were slim. He had a hole in the side of his heart, and a vein that supplies blood to the heart was not connected. I was asked to baptise him. I went into the hospital for the little service with some of his family, and we prayed for his healing. The operation was completely successful and he is now a normal, healthy, mischievous three-year-old. Baptism, like Communion, is a healing sacrament.

2. For Those Who Minister

I offer here some guidelines for those involved in the ministry of prayer for healing with laying on of hands.

Preparing

'Prepare in Prayer' is again the key to involvement in this ministry. Just as Christ's power came through his union with the Father, so too our unity with God – through Christ – is vital, and this is maintained by prayer.

There needs to be as much time as possible given over to prayerful preparation. That prayer must first take the form of a personal preparation. We pray that we might be used as channels of God's healing power. Just as I often feel that I need a bath before going out to a special occasion or event, so too I usually feel that I need a 'spiritual bath' before a service of prayer for healing. I feel that I need to make room for a personal time of confession and cleansing, so that the channel may not be blocked up with anything that is wrong in my life

or attitudes, and then a personal recommitment of myself to
be used in this ministry. It is also important to pray for the
others who will be involved in this ministry, and for those
who will be coming forward at the service, praying both
generally and for those whom we specifically know will be
coming. I have found fasting to be of tremendous value in all
of this – for twenty-four hours before such a service – for it
heightens my awareness of God and my commitment to his
will and the needs of others. Finally, I would commend to
you the suggestion of a day of prayer, which not only offers
everyone the best encouragement for preparation, but also
creates the setting for Christ to come and heal.

Praying for Healing

As we begin to minister to those who come forward for prayer
for healing with laying on of hands, we do so in love and
obedience to God, and in love, compassion and care for those
who are sick. If we do not minister in love, we are of little
use.[1] We need to have a real appreciation of every person's
worth before God, to try to see people as God sees them. It is
then that we can minister in true love without judging,
categorising or condemning others.

As we gently lay hands on a person's head, there are a
number of ways in which we can pray for healing. Some
would focus on the illness and its root-cause, asking God
specifically to heal each troubled part. There are two dangers
with this approach. Firstly, we may not have diagnosed the
problem correctly or reached the real source, and secondly
we can soon become overwhelmed by the weight of sickness
and suffering. Others find it more helpful to focus upon the
person himself in a loving way, perhaps picturing him as
being healed and whole. This is a more positive approach.
However, I believe that the best approach of all is just to
focus upon the love and power of God, in his Son, and to
allow him to heal in his own way. All prayer is addressed
to God, so this seems to me a natural priority, though we may
well choose to mention the particular problem in that prayer.

The manner in which we express our prayers is bound to be affected by the particular approach that we choose. Many prefer spontaneous prayer in response to a person's needs. I generally prefer a set form of words (with occasional variations), as this enables me to focus more specifically on God at the time. When ministering in groups, it is good to have all of these approaches together, though only one needs to speak out aloud. There is no specific method or formula that brings healing, but I believe that it is best to pray to the Father in the name of his Son and by the power of his Holy Spirit. I think it is best too to pray in a quiet, confident voice, without loud or dramatic exhortations.

Most churches seem to minister in pairs – one ordained and one lay. We have always ministered in threes or fours at services (usually in two teams of three or four at a healing service), and sometimes more on other occasions. At the healing service, most of the congregation seem to be especially concerned at the time with their own needs or problems. It is therefore good to have a greater focus of prayer on each of those coming forward. Many who minister in this way experience tingles in arms and fingers. It has been my experience that such feelings do not signify anything at all. It is not necessary to spend very long with each person; a short prayer is quite sufficient. Finally, it is unlikely but none-the-less possible that people may fall to the ground as a result of this ministry. This would not be something to be over-concerned about even though a person may remain 'resting in the Spirit' for up to twenty minutes. This does not signify that healing has actually taken place, though the person usually awakens with a deep sense of peace. Perhaps the greatest concern is that it can become a catching habit!

When we minister to a person in his home or in a group, a more personal approach is probably better, for then we have the time to offer undivided attention, but again there is no need for lengthy prayers of petition.

To minister to the sick in this way is both a privilege and a challenge, but we must never forget that we are just channels through which God's healing power can flow.

For further consideration of the areas covered in this chapter, I would recommend a number of John Richards' pamphlets (see appendix 2).

Notes

1. see I Cor. 13

Chapter 13

PREPARING AND RECEIVING

1. Preparing to Receive

For those involved in Christian healing ministry, preparing people to receive that healing must be an important part of personal ministry. It has been my experience that those who have carefully prepared themselves to receive healing are those most likely to be healed. This chapter offers some thoughts along these lines.

Preparing in Prayer

In many ways the preparation of the person seeking healing is similar to that outlined for those who minister. In the first place, prayer is the most important part of that preparation, and that does not simply involve persistently drawing our request to God's attention.

In prayerfulness, a person needs to try to see himself as God sees him. I suppose it's a bit like looking at the whole of one's life in a mirror, and this includes past, present and future. Few people like what they first see, for it is faults, weaknesses and all kinds of sins that seem to loom largest, even though their roots may be long ago in the past. Yet it is only those who are conscious of their weaknesses whom God can make strong, by their dependence upon him. In these prayers of preparation a person needs to place himself before God, just as he is, and to confess humbly all waywardness, weakness and failings that are in his mind, and to ask God to cleanse him, to make him whole again, to make him strong.

This preparation should gain momentum in the days preceding the service of prayer for healing, especially the day of the service itself. The formal act of confession and absolution should take place prior to the actual prayers for healing in the service. If a person is well enough to fast in any way, this can be a great support, but if in doubt one should check with a doctor beforehand. It is also good to ask for the prayer-support of as many friends and relatives as possible on the day of the service.

Packing up Troubles

For many people, the root of all their problems is what they see as a mountain of worries and troubles. In preparing, they should be encouraged to take each of these worries *without dwelling upon them* and imagine they were packing them up in a bag or parcel, to bring to the service – *and leave there* – in the capable care of Christ. A mass of worries can be a block to healing, for it can cause a person's view of Jesus to be totally obscured.

A Sense of Expectancy

Focussing upon ourselves, our needs, our worries and our problems is only the first part of a person's preparation. It can be both dangerous and depressing to spend most of this time in a totally self-centred manner. The second part of our preparation involves looking to God, for it is when we place all before him, his love and his power, that our needs and our problems seem to diminish.

In looking at the extent of God's power and love, through the Gospels, our sense of expectancy can only be heightened. In reading some of the promises of Jesus a person can begin to appreciate not only what he *can* do for us, but also what he *longs* to do. Healing is his will. The best way to approach the service is in believing not only that Christ still *can* and *does* heal, but that he *will* heal.

Andrea had been suffering from paralytic migraines fo

over a year. She was one of St Mark's teenage members, and this problem had really begun to get her down. The migraines came every ten days or so and affected her in a manner rather like a slight stroke, in that one side of her body would tingle with pins and needles before going numb. We talked through the problem, and Andrea prepared to come to one of the healing services. She came expecting to be healed. Although she experienced nothing at the service itself, she left the church believing that God had healed her there. Two more migraines followed shortly afterwards, but still she believed she had been healed. She had, for they were the last! She received exactly what she had expected to receive and believed she had received.

Putting Ourselves in God's Hands

Finally, a person seeking healing needs to put himself entirely in God's hands. We must come to him as little children, not hesitating to make known our requests, but realising that he knows and will do what is best. Such trust is not easy, and only comes through knowing just whom we are trusting.

We must not prepare with the attitude of trying to make God do what *we* want. We must not try to dictate the terms – the how, where, when and why. God longs to heal and he always knows what is best; it is up to us to make his will our will, and to be open to whatever he wants to give to us.

We need to seek wholeness and if a person prepares in this kind of way, and is then able to make a formal commitment of putting himself in God's hands, then he will not be disappointed. It is this kind of commitment that seems to enable God's healing power to flow right through, bringing a deep sense of peace and wholeness.

Gwen was troubled with an arthritic complaint which had steadily grown worse over a period of four or five years. Her neck was always stiff, she had pains in her right arm and shoulder, and at work and in bed she always had trouble in moving her head. She had been given a surgical collar to wear when the pain was at its worst. She decided to come to one of the healing services, and began to prepare.

She was awoken during the night before the service with a clear feeling of direction from God that she was to put her hand in the hand of Jesus. She came to the service determined to do so, and when she came forward she was able to make that commitment. She returned to her seat and knelt down to thank God, and immediately felt something like an electric shock passing through all the affected areas. She began to shake all over and had to be helped to sit down. Gwen then experienced a warm feeling all over, bringing calm and peace.

She left the church filled with excitement at what had happened and believing that she had been healed. She had been. Apart from a few twinges one day after painting a ceiling, she has not been troubled since.

2. Receiving

Something for Everybody

If we come before the Father in the way I have outlined, as loving children, eager to do his will and knowing that he wants the very best for us, then there is no way that we will come away empty-handed. The Father has something to give to every one of his children, and none will ever be rejected or turned away. We must be clear about this. If a person says that he has received nothing, then it is because he was either unwilling or unable to receive what the Father so much wanted to give to him: probably because his heart was so fixed upon what *he* wanted that he failed to see what *God* was offering. I feel so sad when I see those whom I know could be healed but who either can't or won't receive that healing.

Freda was such a person. She had led a lonely sort of life, for although she had married and raised a family she had never felt loved and appreciated. To list her ailments would fill a page; I will just say that her trips to the doctors were at least weekly, and she felt unable to live without tablets. Her conversation was always only about her catalogue of worries and troubles. Yet she wouldn't let them go; they dominated her life. She just didn't seem able to see the love and the power of God above her troubles and illnesses, and I doubt whether she believed that God wanted to heal her or give her anything. Time and again she would come forward for prayers for healing, but every time she would leave the church still clutching tightly to her bag of troubles and still talking about them. She just couldn't part with them, and their domination of her life obscured completely her view of Christ. I know that there was so much that God longed to give to Freda, but she couldn't even see it. The Father always has something wonderful for every one of his children.

What We Receive

One of the wonders of Christian healing ministry is that we never know quite what we might receive. As you will have seen in these pages, so many people receive far more than they ever imagined. Sheila had suffered from poor circulation ever since she had rheumatic fever as a child. In the winter, whenever she was out in the cold, her fingers would turn white and become numb, which was quite a problem with her having an outdoor job. But she had never thought to ask for healing of that. However, one autumn she came forward at a healing service, not to ask for any specific healing but to lay before God her worries and unload her many burdens. Sheila certainly felt her worries ease, but a few months later she realised she had received something more. She noticed that the cold no longer affected her fingers – she could even throw snowballs again! Perhaps this shows clearly why, when coming forward, it is best just to place ourselves in the Father's caring hands, and then we can accept whatever he wants to give us. Wholeness can be ours.

One of Christ's greatest gifts to us all is the gift of peace.[1] So many people say to me after a healing service that they have experienced a deep sense of peace, even though not all of them have been physically healed. The 'Ring of Peace' and similar forms of meditation are conducive to experiencing this peace. It is a peace that comes from making ourselves at one with the Father's will, from focussing our gaze entirely upon Jesus, from letting go of ourselves and all our problems and resting in his strength. It is a peace which can calm our fears and anxieties, can lift the burdens of all our worries and can heal our many hurts or feelings of guilt. It is a really positive, all-embracing kind of peace, which lifts us very close to God, and can bring healing to the roots of our troubles.

How We Receive

So it is that we can receive by clearing the way to make ourselves completely open to God, by coming forward with open hands and arms. If we can picture the scene of the return of the Lost (or Prodigal) Son,[2] then that is how we make ourselves open to receive. Too often people can feel a need to plead with God and to strive for their healing. There is no need, God already longs to give us the very best. We receive by relaxing in the knowledge of his love and care.

There are five ways in which we receive healing: —

1. We receive by *believing*; believing that the Father longs to, can and will make us whole.
2. We receive by *trusting*; trusting in his love and power and promises.
3. We receive by *submitting*; allowing him to have his way with our lives.
4. We receive by *unburdening*; laying all our troubles at the foot of the cross.
5. We receive by *accepting*; accepting in our lives all that he wants to give to us.

This is how we receive healing and wholeness.

At the time of laying on of hands, it is not uncommon for people to experience unusual feelings or sensations. Some may experience something like an electric shock or current passing through the body; others may mention feelings of warmth or heat, often at the affected points; many comment on feelings of excitement or of energy; others may feel sadness and sometimes tears. These should never be taken as definite signs of physical healing, though they are no doubt signs of God's Holy Spirit at work in our lives and bodies. Most people who are healed experience no such signs at all.

When We Receive

We cannot determine the time when we may experience healing. Some are healed instantly, but most experience their healing either gradually or after a little time. Joan happened to arrive at the vicarage on one of our days of prayer, when there was to be a service of prayer for healing in the evening. She had been troubled for about six weeks by a flicker above her right eye, which was now affecting the eyelid and causing her constant irritation. She came forward at the evening service and, though she experienced a deep sense of peace, the flicker remained. Then, five days later, it just stopped, and she has not been troubled since.

We must trust that God knows best how and when to heal us. Those I have spoken to about gradual and delayed healings seem to appreciate that this was in fact the best way. We might suggest many reasons for this, but they would probably only be guesses. All I would say is that such healings·often leave a more lasting mark on the life of the person who has been healed, as his faith has grown through the experience.

(Many churches find it helpful to offer a leaflet for the guidance of those preparing to receive prayer for healing with laying on of hands. Appendix 3 is a sample of such a leaflet.)

Notes

1. John 14:27
2. Luke 15:20-24

Chapter 14

WALKING OUT ONE'S HEALING

1. Support of the Church

When a person has received prayer for healing with the laying on of hands, this is not the end of the healing process; it is only the beginning. For then a person has to begin to walk on as a healed person, to go out and witness to his healing by God. For this everyone needs the constant support of the local church, its ministers and its fellowship. This going onward is sometimes described as 'walking out one's healing'.

The support that is needed is both individual and corporate. The individual minister needs to be available for support and advice, and must continue to pray for the healed person. Part of his role will be that of encourager, looking out for and pointing out all signs of encouragement, and helping to turn negative doubts into positive expectations. Some will need more support than others, especially those who tend to be pessimistic or who see little evidence of what God has done for them. Help may be needed to discover what God has given, or – if this still cannot be seen – help to understand why! It will also be the minister's task to ensure that the healed person continues firm in his commitment to God.

Here too the fellowship of the local church is vital. A person may need 'family support' in times of challenge, doubt or setback. He will need the church's worship, fellowship and care, for there are many who have drifted from the church and lapsed back into sickness. We walk out our healing by walking close to God.

2. Challenges, Doubts and Setbacks

Challenges

It has been my experience that most people who have been healed can identify a moment of challenge to that healing, when they have been actually faced with the decision of either going on or turning back. These challenges come in two main ways: through a physical challenge to the reality of the healing, or through the (often unkind) words of scepticism from others.

The physical type of challenge can come with some sense of the return of the symptoms of the illness or trouble. It is vital at this point that the person turns immediately to God, to thank him again for the healing, and also to pray that he will remove this threat. If he tries to cope on his own he will fall! The challenges that come through unhelpful 'friends' can be very wounding, and it is here that the support of the fellowship is so vital.

This latter problem is nothing new, as we can see from the story of the blind man whom Jesus healed by the Pool of Siloam.[1] We can learn quite a bit from the way *he* dealt with these doubters. Jesus healed his blindness, and the first thing he did was to affirm his healing and to tell everyone *who* had healed him. Then the religious leaders began their onslaught: first of all his healing was condemned, because it happened on the Sabbath; then the actual healing was questioned; then Jesus himself was declared to be a sinner. The man's constant response to all this was to affirm his healing, and then he began gently to mock the religious leaders. They became angry. They cursed him and tried to belittle him. However, he calmly responded by affirming Jesus' unity with God and his power to heal. This was just too much for them; they couldn't allow such a person to speak to them in this way, and he was expelled from the synagogue for his troubles. Yet he was healed, he had coped with the challenges by affirming his healing and his trust in Christ,

and he could now walk on. I'm sure he felt that his expulsion
from the synagogue was a small price to pay for the return of
his sight. But what an object-lesson for us all in the art of
walking out one's healing. This story makes good reading for
those whose healing is challenged by others.

Doubts

We all have moments of doubt about everything, and healing
will be no exception. An 'old twinge', a moment of depression
or having to cope with some minor calamity; all these things
can bring on doubts about the reality of one's healing. The
ways of coping with such doubts are quite straightforward.

First of all we must always continue to affirm our healing,
and keep on thanking God for it. We must be careful not to
get into the habit of looking back or of thinking too much
about the past illness. If we persistently look back doubts will
begin to grow. We must instead look forward, as a healed
person, and keep on looking to Christ. When any sickness is
laid before his might and power, its strength is diminished.

In time of doubt we must turn immediately to prayer.
There is no need to ask for further healing once we have been
completely healed. All we need to do is to thank God for it,
over and over again.

Setbacks

Occasionally people do suffer setbacks. It is vital that a
person is given urgent and adequate support at this point.
Our first task must be to try to ascertain why the setback has
occurred.

There can be many causes of setbacks beyond those
already mentioned. The most common one is when a person
has drifted from his new-found closeness to God, or perhaps
even drifted from the fellowship of the church too. In a lesser
way, he may just have failed to turn to God for help in his
time of trouble. Another reason for setbacks can be a gradual
slipping back into old ways: starting to worry again, feeling

guilty, doing wrong or whatever was the source of the problem. Setbacks can be caused by people's holding on to resentments or maintaining bad relationships. It is when a person turns away from God, either by drifting or by sinning, that setbacks become most likely. Sometimes the situation can be made worse by trying to cope alone and not turning to the church for help. There is one other important possibility in the list of reasons for setbacks and that is that the root-cause of the trouble has not been healed. We may only have been dealing with the symptoms!

Whatever may be the reasons for a setback, it is important that the ministers of the church are ready and available to help, by prayerfully seeking the reasons for this, by making the person aware of these reasons and then by giving direction and support in dealing with the problem and walking onward.

We must deal with all challenges, doubts and setbacks by keeping close to God and ensuring that we never turn away from him. I find the following verses from the Letter to the Hebrews to be of great guidance in all this:

> Lift up your tired hands, then, and strengthen your trembling knees! Keep walking on straight paths, so that the lame foot may not be disabled, but instead be healed.
> Try to be at peace with everyone, and try to live a holy life, because no one will see the Lord without it. Guard against turning back from the grace of God. Let no one become like a bitter plant that grows up and causes many troubles with its poison (Hebrews 12:12-15 GNB).

3. Walking On in Our Healing

Thanking God

Having been healed, a person needs to walk on in constant thankfulness to God. I believe that there is no better way to do this than by beginning every day – early in the morning –

by offering to God a short prayer of thankfulness. This will make each day a day of thankfulness for that person, and will probably lead to many other daily opportunities to witness to their healing in thankfulness to God.

Most healings are gradual and progressive, and an attitude of constant thankfulness encourages the healing to continue. We need to look for every tiny sign of encouragement, and to affirm our faith by thanking God for it. Most of us feel a bit short on faith, yet it is incredible how quickly our faith can grow as we see God's healing power at work. Then, as our faith grows, so too does our healing. Jim Glennon uses a marvellous biblical analogy by comparing healing with a growing plant in his book *Your Healing is Within You* (see appendix 2).

It is by a constant attitude of positive thankfulness that a person most effectively affirms his healing. That thankfulness will then go on to affect the whole of his life.

Telling the Doctor

Jesus would sometimes send those whom he had healed to the priests. This was in order that they might confirm the healing. Today, many of those who are healed find it difficult or embarrassing to explain to their doctor what has happened to them. However it is important that we walk on in our healing under the direction of our doctor, unless perhaps he is totally sceptical about Christian healing ministry.

Some people may instantly want to throw away tablets in the firm conviction that they have been healed. Others who are being healed gradually may have difficulty in knowing what to do about ongoing medical treatment. I believe that it is important to be totally honest and open with a doctor. If we believe that we have been healed, it is not lack of faith to ask the doctor for an examination to confirm it. Furthermore, mutual respect between the medical profession and those involved in Christian healing ministry is of great importance. Not only should a person go to his doctor for confirmation of the healing, but he should also make it clear that he has been encouraged to do so, and that he respects medical guidance too. There must be no conflict or rivalry. Those who are being healed progressively often need to be under the care and supervision of their doctor in order for him to adjust medical treatment as necessary. The only exception to this guidance comes in encountering a totally sceptical and unhelpful doctor. Then, perhaps a change of doctor might be called for.

So there need be no embarrassment about telling the doctor; it may be our first opportunity (or our first challenge!) to witness to our healing. It is best for a person to describe his healing in the simplest terms – what he *thinks* has happened – and then to leave the doctor to form his own professional opinion. We must avoid putting him in a threatening or defensive position by over-enthusiasm or lack of charity and wisdom. We need to be sensible and honest, taking things steadily, one step at a time, and trusting that God will guide the doctor too.

Walking On

Very often those who have been healed are cured by both medical and spiritual means. In such situations it is important that we give all the glory to God. We may be deeply grateful to doctors and surgeons for their skill and care, or to ministers for their prayer and commitment, but we must acknowledge that all healing comes from God, and so it is to him that all the glory must go. This needs to be a part of our everyday witness of thankfulness as we walk on in our healing.

The Holy Communion is another marvellous support in walking on. Each time a person receives the bread and the wine he is reaffirming his unity with Christ, and Christ can restore him again to wholeness. This is what Communion is all about, and is a right use of the sacrament.

Let me sum up by telling you the story of Carol. She had suffered from migraines ever since starting work some three years previously. She was a tense person who worried a great deal about the slightest upset or error, and was always most concerned that she gave of her best and that her best was good enough. These migraines would occur about once a week, they would last for anything up to twelve hours and they would increase her sense of tension and worry. She had been given tranquillisers and pain-killers to help her to cope with these problems.

After a little chat about the causes of her problems, Carol came with her husband to one of the services of prayer for healing, hopeful that she would indeed be healed. After coming forward for prayer with laying on of hands, both Carol and her husband experienced a deep sense of peace and relaxation as they sat together. But then Carol broke down suddenly in uncontrollable tears which must have lasted for well over fifteen minutes, for she was still sobbing after the service had finished. Afterwards she felt so much better; all her tensions had eased and the migraines were gone. About two weeks later, a colleague at work commented on how much more relaxed she seemed to be. No longer did she get worried and worked up so easily. Three months later she discovered she was pregnant, and right through her pregnancy, and for about a year after her little daughter was born, she walked on confidently in her healing with no more tension or migraines.

However, when I was talking to Carol recently, she admitted that the old feelings of tension were beginning to creep back again. She was also having the odd migraine every few months now. Although her problems were nothing like as severe as they used to be, she realised that she was no longer walking out her healing, and that things were getting worse. Together we carefully searched to find the reasons for this, and discovered that she was starting to become independent again, instead of relying on God for everything. There and then we prayed together that God would lift these worries, help her to grow more dependent upon him again and confirm her in her healing. Once more she was able to set off, walking out her healing.

4. Why We are Healed

Finally, a few important words about why we are healed. We are healed so that we may become whole in every way. We are healed so that we may become better witnesses and servants to the living God of love, whose nature is seen through the Gospels and experienced through the risen Lord, Jesus Christ. We are healed in order to go out and proclaim his love and power to all, that others may seek and find wholeness and fulfilment in their everyday lives. Some of the best ministers and witnesses that we have in our congregation are those who themselves have been wonderfully healed. They are not shy to tell others about it, or to encourage others to seek wholeness themselves. Perhaps the greatest example of all was St Paul!

I close with a quotation from John Richards' pamphlet *Getting Healing Under Way*:

> God does not heal the Church,
>   because the *Church* needs healing.
> He heals the Church,
>   because the *world* needs healing.

> It is important symbolism for me that the action of laying on of hands for healing is identical to the action of the laying on of hands for commissioning and sending-out. The two are inseparable.

> May we go and tell,
>   what good things the Lord has done for us.

Notes

1. John 9:1-34

Appendix 1

SUGGESTIONS FOR GROUP DISCUSSIONS

If you wish to use this book for group study over a period of weeks, the questions below are offered as a means of opening up useful discussion concerning the areas covered in the chapters. The sharing of personal experiences and feelings should be encouraged, for this is always the first step on the road towards the development of a deep sense of trust and caring within a group. This is part of the foundation needed for Christian healing ministry. The other vital part is prayer, and each meeting should always close with a time of open prayer together. The one danger to beware of is that a group can easily become introverted. I hope the questions will discourage this.

Chapters 2 & 3

The group might best begin by simply discussing reactions to some of the main events outlined in these two chapters, such as the day of prayer or the service of prayer for healing; how it was used, comparisons with your own church situation, etc.

Chapter 4

1. How can we be sure of God's love and care for all our needs, however small, of his power to heal and of his will to heal?
2. Does the fact of sickness in our everyday world cause us to doubt God's love and power to heal? Why doesn't he just get rid of it all?
3. How was it that Jesus could always see immediately the root-cause of a person's sickness, and heal it?

4. Consider why Jesus regarded sickness as he did, and what this tells us about the nature of the Father.
5. Consider how we are called to respond to the Father's love.

Chapter 5

1. Consider reasons for the prominence of prayer for healing in the ministry of the early Church.
2. How did that ministry begin and develop?
3. Why did it decline and fade in later years?
4. Consider whether the revival of Christian healing ministry in the twentieth century is a good thing or not.
5. What part and place should Christian healing ministry have in the life of the local church today?

Chapter 6

1. What evidence is there, within your church fellowship, of loving care for the sick and expectant prayer for their healing?
2. How might this be further developed?
3. What steps might be taken to prepare for the development of a formal ministry of prayer for healing?
4. What difficulties might be encountered, and how can they be anticipated and dealt with?
5. If this has not already begun, should prayers for the healing of the sick now be a part of each meeting?

Chapter 7

1. In what ways can we grow together in faith and dependency upon the Father?
2. How do we rightly ask God to heal?
3. How important is the faith of the sick person?
4. How can we cope with our doubts and fears?
5. How can we know and see that God has responded to our prayers?

Chapter 8

1. Consider some of the main causes of stress today, and how they affect *us*.

2. How important to our health are our relationships, our attitudes and our moral standards?
3. Consider what steps we might take to develop a healthier lifestyle.
4. Consider the medical opinion that between fifty and ninety per cent of all illnesses have emotional causes.
5. What is wholeness?

Chapter 9

1. Consider how past experiences and relationships have made *us* the people we are.
2. Consider how our present situations can become prisons.
3. What are our personal fears for the future, and how large do they loom in our lives?
4. How might we begin to pray together for the healing of past experiences?
5. Provided that a real sense of trust has developed within the group, members might be able to discuss in twos or threes how each sees him/herself and is seen by others. This will need to be done with gentle truthfulness and sensitivity!

Chapter 10

1. How can we ourselves cope with non-healings?
2. How can we best respond to those who have not yet been healed?
3. How can we try to find out why a person has not been healed?
4. Is it right to keep on praying for those not yet healed?
5. How can we encourage and support those who suffer?

Chapters 11 & 12

1. What is the role of the priest/minister/pastor?
2. Discuss ways in which pastoral ministry can and should be shared.
3. Consider the practices of prayer for healing with laying on of hands and anointing, and their current re-emergence as a vital part of pastoral ministry.
4. Consider how best healing ministry might be introduced in your church.
5. The group might roughly plan a service of prayer for healing.

Chapters 13 & 14

1. Consider ways to prepare to receive prayer for healing with laying on of hands.
2. How can we, as a church, help those who have been healed to see and walk in their healing?
3. How can we best help them to cope with challenges, doubts and setbacks?
4. How can we encourage them to share with others the fact of their healing?
5. Consider why people are healed.

During these sessions the group is likely to want to 'experiment' with prayer for healing, with laying on of hands etc. Provided that this has been carefully and fully discussed and agreed with the minister or pastor, then it should be encouraged. However, it must come about naturally without any 'looking around for likely customers'!

Appendix 2

SOME USEFUL RESOURCES

BOOKS

Christian Healing Ministry

The Christian Healing Ministry – Morris Maddocks (S.P.C.K. 1981)
Healing – Francis MacNutt (Ave Maria 1974)
Your Healing is Within You – Jim Glennon (Hodder 1978)
How Can I Find Healing? – Jim Glennon (Hodder 1984)
Heal the Sick – Reginald East (Hodder 1977)
Christian Healing Rediscovered – Roy Lawrence (Kingsway 1976)
Invitation to Healing – Roy Lawrence (Kingsway 1979)
We Believe in Healing – Ed. Ann England (Marshalls 1982)
The Gift of Inner Healing – Ruth Carter Stapleton (Word 1976)

Prayer, Fasting, Counselling, Shared Ministry

The Prayer Principle – Michael Baughen (Mowbrays 1981)
God's Chosen Fast – Arthur Wallis (Victory 1968)
A Friend in Need – Selwyn Hughes (Kingsway 1981)
I Believe in the Church – David Watson (Hodder 1978)

BOOKLETS AND PAMPHLETS

Ministry to the Sick – Anglican Authorised Alternative Services.
Wholeness and Healing – Bishop of Liverpool's Panel on the Ministry of Healing (available from: Liverpool Diocesan Publishing Company, Church House, 1 Hanover Street, Liverpool L1 3DW).

The Church's Healing Ministry ⎫
Getting Healing Under Way ⎪
Why Am I Not Healed ⎬   – All by John Richards
'Resting in the Spirit' ⎪
Laying on of Hands ⎪
Understanding Anointing ⎭

(All John Richards' writings are available from: Renewal Servicing, P.O. Box 366, Addlestone, Weybridge, Surrey.)

PRAYERS

Prayer for the Commissioning of Those Administering Laying on of Hands:

N,   may the healing power of the Holy Spirit be in you. Amen.

Prayers for Healing with Laying on of Hands:

N,   may the Lord Jesus Christ, in his great love for you, make you whole in every way; and so may you grow in faith and in love, by the power of his Holy Spirit. Amen.

N,   we lay hands on you in the name of the Father and of the Son and of the Holy Spirit, that you may know the healing power of our Lord Jesus Christ, and be made whole by him. Amen. (See also *Ministry to the Sick* – Anglican Alternative Services.)

Prayers for the Blessing of Oil:

Heavenly Father, you brought healing to the sick through your Son, Jesus Christ. Send your Holy Spirit to bless and sanctify this oil, which nature has provided to serve the needs of men. May your blessing come upon all who are anointed with this oil, that they may be freed from pain, illness and disease, and made well again in body, mind and soul. Amen.

O Lord, holy Father, giver of health and salvation, send your Holy Spirit to sanctify this oil, that, as your holy Apostles anointed many who were sick and healed them, so may those who in faith and repentance are anointed with this oil be made whole in every way, through your Son, our Saviour, Jesus Christ. Amen.

Prayers of Anointing with Laying on of Hands:

N,   I anoint you with oil in the name of the Father, and of the Son and of the Holy Spirit. As you are outwardly anointed with this holy oil, so may our heavenly Father grant you the inward anointing of the Holy Spirit. In his great mercy may he forgive your sins, release you from suffering and restore you to wholeness and strength. May he deliver you from all evil, preserve you in all goodness and bring you to everlasting life; through Jesus Christ, our Lord. Amen.

N,   I anoint you with oil in the name of the Father and of the Son and of the Holy Spirit. Through this holy anointing and the laying on of hands, may the Lord Jesus Christ, in his great love for you, forgive your sins and make you whole in every way, and so may you grow in faith and in love, by the power of his Holy Spirit. Amen.
(See also *Ministry to the Sick* – Anglican Alternative Services.)

Appendix 3

PREPARING, RECEIVING, AND WALKING ON

For those who seek prayer for healing, with laying on of hands.
Some helpful Bible verses:
Luke 11:9-13.
James 5:13-16.
John 10:10(b).
The various healing miracles of Jesus.

Preparing

Those who have carefully prepared themselves to receive healing are usually those most likely to be healed. These thoughts are offered to help in this.

Preparing in Prayer

Prayer is the most important part of preparing. This does not just involve drawing your request to God's attention; but more important, kneeling before him, admitting all your faults and weaknesses, and asking God to cleanse you, and to make you whole and strong in every way. Some find it helpful to fast, by going without food (not drink) for up to twenty-four hours before the service.

Packing up Troubles

If you are a worrier, or if you feel you have more than your share of troubles at present, it is a good idea to take each of your concerns, *without dwelling on them*, and imagine that you are packing them up in a bag or parcel. Then you can bring them to the service, *and leave them there*, in the capable hands of Christ.

Growing in Expectancy

Whilst one part of the preparation involves looking at yourself (as in a mirror), the other part is looking to God – for it is when you place all before his loving power that your needs and your problems can begin to diminish.

In reading some of Jesus' healing miracles in the New Testament, and some of his promises too, you can begin to appreciate not only what he *can* do for you, but also what he longs to do. Healing is his will. The best way to approach the service is in believing not only that Christ still *can* and *does* heal, but that he *will* heal.

Putting Ourselves in God's Hands

You need to realise and accept that God, as your loving Father, knows and will do what is best. Rather than trying to make God do what you want, it is best just to put yourself entirely in his hands.

Receiving

Something for Everyone

As our loving Father, God wants the very best for all his children, and there is no way that anyone would be turned away empty-handed. He has something for everyone, but you must be sure that your heart is not so fixed upon what *you* want, that you fail to see and accept what God is offering you.

What We Receive

One of the wonders of Christian healing ministry is that you never know quite what you might receive. Some receive far more than they would have imagined!

One of Christ's greatest gifts to us all is the gift of peace, and many experience that peace with prayers for healing. It is a peace that comes from being at one with the Father's will, from letting go of yourself and all your problems and resting in his strength and love. It is an all-embracing peace which calms fears and anxieties, heals hurts and pains, and lifts you very close to God, bringing healing to the roots of your troubles.

How We Receive

We receive by *believing* – believing that the Father longs to, can, and will make us whole.

We receive by *trusting* – trusting in his love and power and promises.

We receive by *submitting* – by allowing him to have his way with our lives.

We receive by *unburdening* – by laying all our troubles at the foot of the cross.

We receive by *accepting* – by accepting in our lives all that he wants to give to us.

When We Receive

While some are healed instantly, most experience their healing either gradually or after a little time. It is never easy to be patient, yet we must trust that God knows best how and when to heal.

Walking On

Thanking God

Having been healed, a person needs to walk on in constant thankfulness to God. It is best to begin each day with a prayer of thankfulness to God. Most healings are gradual, and such an attitude of thankfulness enables healing to continue and grow. You need to look for every tiny sign of encouragement, and to affirm your faith by thanking God for it.

Telling the Doctor

Christian healing ministry is neither opposed to nor an alternative to medical treatment. There need be no embarrassment about telling the doctor – just explain your healing in the simplest terms, what you *think* has happened, and then leave the doctor to form his own professional opinion.

Challenges, Doubts and Setbacks

Most people who have been healed can identify moments of challenge to that healing. Sometimes they come in the form of doubts or setbacks. At other times they may be a result of the (often unkind) scepticism of other people.

At such times you must turn immediately to prayer. There is no need to ask for further healing. Just keep on thanking God for the healing you have already received – over and over again.

Why We are Healed

We are healed so that we might become whole in every way.

We are healed so that we might become better witnesses and servants to the living God of Love.

We are healed in order to go out and proclaim his love and power to all – that others too may seek and find wholeness and fulfilment in their everyday lives.